Julia Doherty

Online Marketing for Small Businesses

In easy steps is an imprint of In Easy Steps Limited
16 Hamilton Terrace · Holly Walk · Leamington Spa
Warwickshire · United Kingdom · CV32 4LY
www.ineasysteps.com

Notice of Liability
Every effort has been made to ensure that this book contains accurate
and current information. However, In Easy Steps Limited and the
author shall not be liable for any loss or damage suffered by readers
as a result of any information contained herein.

Trademarks
All trademarks are acknowledged as belonging to their respective
companies.

Acknowledgements from the author
I wish to thank everyone who helped me complete this book. Without
their continued efforts and support, I would have not been able to
bring my work to a successful completion.
Social Media Gurus such as Michael Stelzner, Pat Flynn, Michael Hyatt
and Gary Vaynerchuk for their valued expertise.
My daughter Rachel Mumford, husband Matt Mumford and mum
Linda Waters for their continued support and patience throughout the
creation of the book.
My work colleagues, clients, Facebook friends and In Easy Steps for
their on-going advice and perseverance with me during my steep
learning curve of my very first book.

In Easy Steps Limited supports The Forest Stewardship Council (FSC),
the leading international forest certification organisation. All our titles
that are printed on Greenpeace approved FSC certified paper carry the
FSC logo.

MIX
Paper from
responsible sources
FSC® C020837

Printed and bound in the United Kingdom

ISBN 978-1-84078-628-6

Contents

9 Google Analytics   257

Index   261

1 An introduction to social media

Why social media is important

Social media has exploded in recent years. We have now entered the age of the relationship. With the help of social media, marketing has evolved into a two-way dialogue, not just a monologue. By using social media as a way to advertise for your company, you can speak directly to the consumers in an arena they are comfortable with. Social media allows businesses to connect with their customers and prospects while shaping their perceptions of products and services.

Social media can be extremely powerful for business. But it can also be a big risk as well. Social media is not your super hero, and if your service is weak, your products are poor, and you do not respond quickly enough to those business failures, then your customers will use social media to enhance and vocalize those feelings for the world to see. Not being online does not take the problem away. Customers will still air their issues online, you just need to make sure that you are also online, and implementing a listening strategy so you can nip any grievances in the bud quickly and efficiently before the problem escalates.

Beware

People will talk about you and your business, whether you are on social media platforms or not.

Hot tip

Set up a listening strategy for your company name.

So, we start this book with setting up an effective listening strategy for your company and your personal name and the rest of the book covers creating an active presence online.

Set up an effective listening strategy

Google Alerts is not the same as it used to be, and it is likely that it will eventually be another tool that Google will terminate, in a similar way that they switched off so many excellent Google products such as Google Reader etc. In addition, Google Alerts only sends you email if new articles, web pages or blog posts make it into the top 10 Google News results, the top 20 Google Web Search results or top 10 Google Blog Search results for your query. If the top results remain the same for a while, you will not receive emails on your topic. For this reason, there's a great product called "Mention", which will monitor and listen to what is being said about you or your company online.

Google Alerts will soon be a thing of the past.

How to get started with Mention

Go to the homepage (**www.mention.net**) and click the **Sign up** button. You can sign up using your existing Facebook, Twitter, Google, or Open ID account, or just enter your name, email address, and a password to create a new account.

Create your free account	Close
Full Name	Do you already have an account on one of these sites?
E-mail Address	🔵 Sign up with Facebook
Password	🔵 Sign up with Twitter
Confirm Password	🔵 Sign up with your Google account
By signing up, you accept the **terms of use** and **privacy policy**	🔵 Sign up with your OpenID
Create your Free account	

If you sign up using an existing account, you'll be asked to enter an email address. Then you can choose how to use Mention.

You can download Mention for Windows, get the app for iPhone or Android, install a Chrome extension (see page 10), or just use the web app.

Register with **mention.net** to perfect your listening strategy.

...cont'd

What is a Google Chrome Extension?

Google Chrome extensions are like mini applications (similar to the apps that you would install on your smartphone). You can access software quickly and easily by simply clicking on the extensions from your Google Chrome bar.

Creating a new alert on Mention

Once you click through to the web app, you'll see a screen where you can create your alert.

Then just complete the form:

Name your alert: I suggest creating a Mention alert for your name, with a second one for your company name. In time, you may want to set up alerts for industry news, your competitors, your product names, etc.

Include and exclude expressions: Type in the words or phrases that you want to get alerts for. You can include common misspellings or variations, and you can also exclude terms, i.e. tell Mention not to send you alerts for pages that include a given word or phrase. For example, there is a very active Twitterer who has the same name as mine, so I have excluded all of her Tweets from my summary email.

Choose your languages: English is the default, but you can choose to receive alerts in French, Spanish, German and many other languages too.

In the next step, you can manage and filter your sources. You could receive alerts from all sources (the web, Facebook, Twitter, news, blogs, videos, forums and images) but you can exclude some of those sources if you wish, or block a specific site.

Hot tip

Set up alerts for your competitors' names and industry news.

11

Manage and filter your sources

Select sources, block specific URLs, activate the Priority filter and trash unwanted mentions thanks to the anti-noise technology.

SOURCES		BLOCKED SITES	
Web	✓	URL	+
Facebook	✓	New mentions coming from these URLs will be blocked and ignored	
Twitter	✓	TECHNOLOGIES	
News	✓	Priority Inbox	✓
Blogs	✓	You can activate the 'Priority' filter. This filter will classify mentions coming from influential people and important sources.	
Videos	✓		
Forums	✓	Anti-Noise Technology	✓
Images	✓	You can activate anti-noise technology. If you want the application to automatically remove mentions similar to those you trash. This technology helps fight against unwanted noise that comes from spam and fraudsters.	

Previous step   Create my alert

On this screen you can also choose whether you want to use "Priority inbox" (a feature that flags Mentions they identify as

...cont'd

more important or influential) and "Anti-Noise Technology" (which removes Mentions similar to those you have deleted).

Then click **Create my alert**. At this point, you can choose to share your alert with other users. Anyone can then see the alerts, but you'll be the owner with the ability to edit and manage settings, add or delete users as well as delete the alert.

Mention notifications

Google Alerts are bare-bones emails with links to the pages that mention the word or phrase you're monitoring. They look at bit like this:

Mention also sends you an email when you have new results:

As you can see, the Mention email is much more user friendly and it also has more options: Click the blue button to go to the page, or click one of the links below the entry to react to the Mention, mark as a favorite or delete the Mention. Clicking any of these links opens up the Mention web app, which looks a lot like an email application, which most users are familiar with.

Hot tip

Utilize the priority inbox feature.

In the far left column, you have a list of views. The default view is Mentions, which you can see in the next column over, with the most recent Mention at the top.

You can filter the Mentions column by source and toggle the view between all, unread, and priority. (The "priority" Mentions have red flags.)

On the right, in the main view, you get a preview of the page with your Mention. This is really cool because you can see the context of the Mention without having to actually visit the page – it's obviously much more robust than the little search-style snippet you get in the Google Alert email. From this view you can choose to click through to the original URL or the source, and you can also "favorite" the Mention, block the source or trash it using the little icons at the top.

Is there a cost to Mention?

At the time of going to print, there is a basic free account for one user, one alert and to receive 100 Mentions a month, and various packages from a premium, business package to a full enterprise bespoke package. Visit **https://en.mention.net/pricing** to find the latest prices.

Hot tip

There is a free version of Mention, but you can pay to upgrade for additional features.

Four steps to online marketing success

It is interesting to see what people consider to be the steps to social media success. Some people just see the numbers. For example, they look at a Twitter account that has 20,000 followers, or they view a Facebook page that has thousands of likes and they assume that they are successful in their social media activities. This not quite true! Social media is successful if you are communicating and building relationships with your target market, which will ultimately convert into new business. There is no point in a kitchen designer from Northamptonshire, UK, having 3,000 likes on their Facebook page, if those likes are all from people in the USA.

Social media success will rarely happen overnight. When you break it down, there are really only four steps to achieve social media success online:

 Build your platforms

The phrase from the *Field of Dreams* film with Kevin Costner, "If you build it, he will come" is so overused nowadays. But there is no getting away from the fact that if your platforms are not professionally designed, if you have an inactive or poorly designed website, or have not bothered to change your Twitter skin then this will have an effect on your overall strategy.

2 Grow your network

It is a well-known fact that if you do not have a network of people to talk to online, then you are really just talking to yourself! Have a strategy for growing your network online for each platform. Decide and define who your target market is and start to follow them. Use tools such as **www.followerwonk.com** to find people on Twitter. Check out LikeAlyzer (see page 120) or run some adverts on Facebook to see how to grow your audience.

The best results we have had was to run an email marketing campaign to tell people about our Company

Social media is not a numbers game.

Review your platforms at least once every six weeks.

LinkedIn page. Make sure that your strategy is ongoing and reviewed at least every six weeks. These tools will be covered in more detail later in the book, as well as giving you more inspirational ideas on how to build your following, connections and likes.

3 ### Define a listening, engagement and content strategy

This is probably the area where most businesses fail on online marketing. Their posts are all over the place, with no consistency. They fail to set up listening strategies to respond to people who are talking about them online (good and bad). Try **mention.net** (see pages 9-13) which has a free service to help you listen to your audience. The scattergun approach to producing content does not work.

Make sure that you are using a social media management system such as Hootsuite (**www.hootsuite.com**) or Tweetdeck (**www.tweetdeck.com**) and start planning what you are going to say and do. Decide on a blogging topic for the month and plan what you are going to write about, with set dates for publication.

But the most important strategy in Step 3 is the word "engagement". Thank people for mentioning you in a Tweet, ask people questions, comment on others' posts etc. You must talk to people in order to build those important relationships that lead to business and referrals.

4 ### Measure the results

As with any type of marketing, whether it is printing leaflets, your website activity, special offers etc., you need to measure the results, and social media activity is no different. If you don't know what is working and what is not working then how do you know if it is successful?

Hot tip

Plan your content topics in advance. Write the topics down for each month and then gear your content posts around those topics.

Don't forget

Don't forget the word "social". It is important to engage and talk to others online for a successful social media strategy.

...cont'd

Remember Einstein's famous quote:

> *Insanity: doing the same thing over and over again and expecting different results.*
>
> albert einstein

It makes good business sense to make sure that you are measuring your activities.

Each chapter of the book will end with a conclusion. For each platform we will declare how to achieve the four steps to social media success, including how to measure your success on each platform, in more specific detail.

Hot tip

Check your Google Analytics (see pages 258-260) to see how much traffic is being generated by your social media activities. You may be pleasantly surprised. Simply click **Acquisition**, then **Social** to view the results.

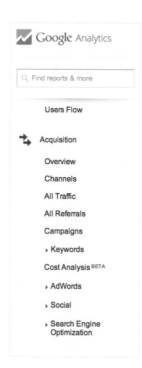

Set your social media goals

So many companies are "winging it" when it comes to social activity. The expressions "Social media ROI" has many names – for example, "return on investment", "return on influence" to name a few, but do you really know what you are trying to achieve by having an effective social media strategy?

Where do you start and how do you relate what to measure online with your overall business goals?

We will discuss 10 reasons that businesses, small and large, are active online. Read through each goal and then choose just two of those goals before you indulge in the rest of this book. Once you decide where you are going, you will have a better vision of how you are going to get there.

Most people will answer the question "Why are you doing social media?" with "To get more sales". Many of the reasons below will result in more sales. Therefore, this has been removed as a reason to be active online.

To drive traffic to your website

If the majority of your sales come from your website, then it is a no-brainer to have this goal as top of your list. Traffic to your website is important for all businesses, but especially important if you are selling your products or services online.

You can create an amazing website that looks stunning, and is extremely functional. However, without traffic to the site, you are going nowhere fast.

Using social media to drive traffic to your website is easy.

You can embed the link to your website in a Tweet.

> **ISV Software Ltd** @ISVSoftwareLtd · Jul 30
> 80% of women feel their employer is supportive of them but 44% say their gender has hindered their career - ow.ly/zzBeH

Check out Chapter 5 for help with Twitter.

Hot tip

Setting your social media goals and objectives is the first stage to social media success.

Hot tip

Use a URL shortener (see pages 144-145) to gain statistics on how often a link has been clicked on from your social networking sites.

...cont'd

In Chapter 4, we will talk through how to post a link to your website on Facebook, which is also a highly effective way to drive traffic back to your website. You can also use the Facebook applications or Facebook adverts to achieve similar results.

Connections Employment Agency Limited shared a link.
3 hours ago

New Job
Warehouse Operative / Counterbalance FLT Driver - Trafford Park, Trafford Park, England, £16000 per annum

Warehouse Operative / Counterbalance FLT Driver - Trafford Park
Warehouse Operative/Counterbalance FLT Driver job in

Posting updates into your LinkedIn status update to drive traffic back to your blog, products online or any part of your website. We'll cover this in Chapter 6.

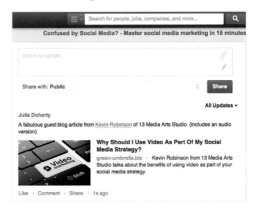

There are many ways in which you can use social media to drive traffic back to your website. Always check that your website is visible in the "About us" areas of your online profiles or biographies online for additional opportunities.

To appear as an expert in your field

Everybody trusts an expert. And, as every salesperson will tell you, individuals want to do business with people they know, like and trust.

The best way to brand yourself as an expert is by using a strategy that leverages social media. This includes LinkedIn, Twitter,

Facebook, YouTube and top of the pile is blogging. We will go into more detail in Chapter 3 on how you can appear as an expert in your field within each platform.

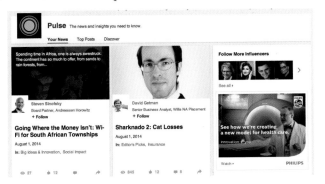

Did you know that you can now become a published author on LinkedIn and become a LinkedIn Influencer? What a fabulous way to appear as an expert in your field! All influencers can be found in the Pulse area of LinkedIn. (Explained in more detail within the LinkedIn chapter).

Brand awareness

There are many reasons that brand awareness may be top of your social media goals. You may be a fledgling company that is dipping its toes in the business world, or you may have been established for many years with a solid customer base, which is now looking to expand into different markets. Perhaps you have a new product to launch, or a new service to a niche market.

Reputation management

Social media helps a brand reach out to their customers and communicate with them, playing a significant role in online reputation management. 70% of people who look for reviews online trust posts by friends and family, while 90% trust reviews from other consumers. From a business-to-business point of view, 42% of people look up the people that they are going to do business with and 45% of people learnt something from searching online which changed their minds. *(Source: http://likedyou.com/category/social/)* What better place to be constantly looking for reviews than social media?

Surveys *(http://ow.ly/tt6Mw)* tell us that 22% of people who have had a bad experience are likely to comment about it online while only 9% of people who have had a good experience will

Don't forget to give away your knowledge and expertise as much as possible to gain credibility.

Provide videos on YouTube to show your expertise in a particular subject, sector or industry.

Make sure all your platforms are branded professionally.

19

...cont'd

do the same. All these numbers point to a growing trend where the reputation of a business online directly impacts bottom line revenue.

Having a strategy for reputation management is key for many businesses, especially in the service industry. Perhaps you have bought a business from a previous owner who did not have a brilliant reputation, in which case having "reputation management" as your main social media goal should be top of your list.

To keep an eye on your competition

If it is important to find out what kind of customers your competition are targeting, or what their social media marketing strategy looks like, then reason number five should be towards the top of your list.

As important as it is to keep an eye on the competition, many small business owners don't know much about what their competitors are doing to reach customers. The benefits of watching your competitors are almost immediate, you learn what you can do to make your business unique, you see their weaknesses (i.e. customer service issues) and you get great ideas to improve your own strategy.

You can set up Twitter lists for all of your competitors (see the Twitter section on pages 136-140 on how to set up lists).

It is easy to keep an eye on your competition on Facebook by clicking the **Get Notifications** button so you do not miss any posts. Once you have done this, for any posts that appear on their page, you will see a red notification symbol on your personal profile.

Don't forget you do not need to actually follow your competitors on Twitter, you simply add them to a list.

Currently, you have no option but to "like" your competitor's page if you would like to subscribe to their Facebook notifications. This will publicly notify both your own network and your competitor of your actions.

Uncover new opportunities and meet new people

Expanding your customer base has always been expensive, and it may be even more so today. In an uncertain economic climate, few companies seem ready to take the risk of starting out with new suppliers. Instead, it makes sense to look for new opportunities in industries where you are already doing business.

If new sales are top of your list, then this goal should be your number one. Your social media strategy for uncovering new opportunities will be based on listening and engagement.

There are endless strategies to gain opportunities for potential new sales. These are covered in the detailed chapters for each platform later in the book.

Customer loyalty

If you are struggling to retain customers, and find yourself having to search for new clients, then customer loyalty will be important to you. Implement a social media strategy to ensure customer retention and loyalty.

There are endless ways to keep in contact with your customers online.

- Make sure that you are tagging your customers in posts that are relevant to them. Here is an example of how you can do this on Facebook:

Tag the business in the post

Green Umbrella Social Media for Business
19 March

This afternoon we have Liz from T E A M for Independent Recruitment

- Feed your customers with regular free content utilizing your blog and social networking platforms.
- Set up Twitter lists for your current clients.
- You can tag your clients in all platforms, to say that it was good to meet with them, or Retweet their messages to your network, share their blog articles on your LinkedIn page, etc.

Don't forget

Remember to use the tagging facility on all networks to ensure that your customer will see the post.

...cont'd

● Have a listening strategy set up for potential customer complaints so that you can react quickly. Providing a first class service online will always help with customer retention.

Get news instantaneously

If you are a local business, then having a listening strategy for local news is key for any business. You may be in an industry that constantly needs to be ahead of the game to be successful. Therefore, this is the goal for you.

● Are you following your local newspapers and radio stations online?
● Do you have notifications set up for your local town?

To help improve your search results

Search remains the main way in which many people discover a business and Search Engine Optimization (SEO) should be a key part of your online communications strategy. An active presence on social media, sharing and distributing keyword-rich content will improve your placing on Google and other search engines, ensuring that more people find you online (see pages 31-32).

Social media is the future of communications

Social media is not a fad and it is not going away. The Net Generation – your next pool of employees, customers, and competitors – prefer to use text messaging and the social web over any other form of communication. It is the natural evolution of communications. If you are not involved in social media at this stage, then you will simply be playing catch-up in a few years' time or your business will not exist.

The social web is where a generation is going to connect, learn and discover. Ignore this at your peril! You have got to be in it to win it! Here are some examples of what we do:

Facebook

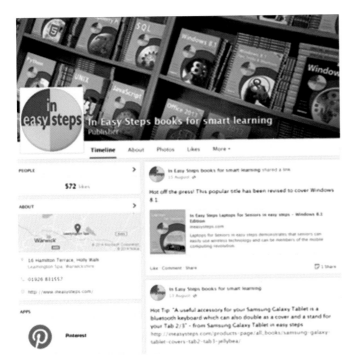

Twitter

...cont'd

Website

Pinterest

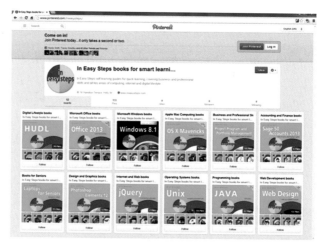

LinkedIn

2 Is your website working for you?

Is your website working for you?

When setting your social media goals and objectives, it is likely that a good percentage of businesses would have ticked "drive traffic to my website" as one of their top goals. The question is, once you have a solid social media presence and you are driving traffic back to your website, you need to ask yourself, "What are people seeing when they land on my site?"

You could have the most expensive website in the world that looks amazing from a design or technical point of view, but you're still not achieving those all important conversions that a small business owner needs. However, there are just 10 key features that your website needs to make it work from a marketing perspective.

Have a look at your own website and see what your score is out of 10 from the following list.

Calls to action

A call to action seems like quite a vague term but, in simple terms, it means that you need to get your visitors to "do something" as soon as they land on the site, and they will need help deciding what to do. When I am analyzing a website, I am looking for key target words such as **download**, **follow**, **click**, **join**, **subscribe**, **call**, **contact**, **free helpline**, etc. These are the words that make a real difference to those all-important conversions.

Here is a homepage that has some great calls to action:

Hot tip

Use effective language on your website to engage your visitors to take action.

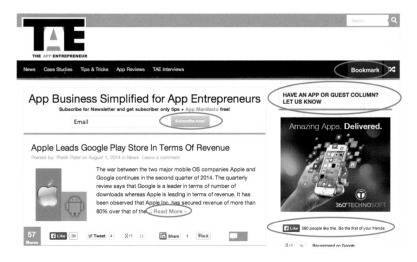

These are subtle, but effective. These actions solidify the relationship with the visitor and the business.

Keep it simple!

As a lead generation tool, it is imperative that you keep your call to action as simple as possible. This is the same on all platforms such as email marketing, press releases, blog posts, social media updates, etc. It is the easiest way to manipulate people's behavior in the way you want. Call to action buttons have varied purposes, and thus a lot of thought and consideration needs to go into deciding what the call to action button aims to achieve.

Be careful and do not overload your homepage with too many calls to action. Make them subtle, with a focus on one or two main call to actions.

What is your "You to We" ratio?

Use customer focused words within the content of your site.

As natural sales people, we feel that we want to tell the whole world about how good we are, how wonderful our products are, and the fabulous customer service that we offer. But visitors to your website only care about how you can help them meet their requirements. For this exercise, change hats and step into the shoes of a potential new customer that is visiting your website, whilst thinking about the following well known saying:

> *To sell John Brown,*
> *What John Brown buys,*
> *You must see the world*
> *Through John Brown's eyes.*
>
> Unknown

So now it is your turn to have a look at your own website and be honest. It's time to ask yourself the following questions:

Is it very obvious what your business does?

Is the site easy to navigate?

Does my site pass the We to You test?

What is the "We to You" test?

1 Look at the opening paragraph on your website and count how many company- or brand-focused words there are. Words such as "we", "our", "us" and your own business name

2 Next, count the number of customer-focused words such as "you" and "your"

3 Take the number of customer-focused words, divide it by the total number of words you counted up, then multiply the answer by 100, to get the percentage

Ideally the ratio should be at least balanced, or leaning in the direction of the customer. If you have an unhealthy ratio, then be aware that in the eyes of your visitor, the business invariably comes across as bragging at its readers, instead of talking to them. If your site is a bit "we-we-we", then I strongly suggest having a look at the content.

This is not an exact science, and I'm certainly not saying that "we" is a bad word, but when you use it, it's far better if you are talking about yourself in the context of that all-important "you" – your customer.

> **So how did you score on the "You to We" ratio? If you were more focused on your customer then award yourself a point in this section.**

Refreshed content or blog

This is discussed in more detail in the blogging chapter. However, before you dismiss adding a blog or news to your website, then let's explain, in very basic terms, how Google ranks a website. If "driving traffic to your website" was top of your goals list, then this section will be relevant to you and your business.

So, how does Google work?

100% S.E.O /Keywords/Meta tags/Link Baiting.

Back in the olden days (in 2009!), the main way of reaching page one in Google was to manipulate your website (called SEO or Search Engine Optimization). This meant that you would spend a lot of time, money and effort adding keywords, metatags, meta descriptions, link baiting and lots of other very technical terms that most people do not understand.

In June 2010, Google decided to change the rules and announced to the world that no longer can you manipulate the system by simply optimizing your website.

With the introduction of the project known as Google Caffeine, there were now **three key elements** involved if you wanted to be successful in Google. Although Caffeine has been updated numerous times, (Panda, Penguin, Hummingbird, etc.), the fundamentals are still the same.

Beware

SEO tactics are not the only ingredient that Google looks for nowadays.

Go₀gle

June 2010
Caffeine, Panda,
Penguin, Hummingbird

Optimize your website

It is still important to make sure that your website is keyword rich and that your designers have optimized your site before submitting it to search engines. However, nowadays, it is not the "be all and end all" of everything. There are two other elements to making sure that you have a chance in ranking in Google.

Creating buzz

Google (and other search engines) is no longer just looking at your website in order to give it a rating in the algorithm. Its spiders or robots are looking all over the Internet to see if you are a good business worthy of being sent up the rankings. Google is everywhere. It is looking in open forums, on social networking platforms, blogging platforms, online newspapers, etc. If your business is being spoken about, or your content is being shared, then you will see a rise in the search engine listings. It is your responsibility to make your business and your content as popular as possible. If you look at the dates that Google Caffeine was released (June 2010), it now makes sense as to why it is important to have a presence online, outside of your website. Having a social media presence is more important than it has ever been.

Having a social media presence is an important ingredient to your search engine optimization within Google.

Refreshed content

The biggest slice of the pie for Google influence is new, fresh, unique content. This is approximately 55% towards the algorithm. Let's explain.

Google will send its spiders or robots to have a look at your website. It will then collect all that good, juicy information and keywords and send it back to Google so that it can be indexed. A few weeks later, Google will resend those spiders back to your website, but this time it will only be collecting any new information on your site. That new information is then sent back to Google for ranking. But what happens if there is no new information on your website? Well, Google thinks to itself, "This company hasn't updated its site, so I will send my spiders back in four weeks' time to check". When the spiders come back in four weeks' time, and there is still no new information on the site, Google will say "No new information, I will send my spiders back in three months' time", and so the cycle continues.

Adding a blog to your website is an easy way to regularly create fresh content.

...cont'd

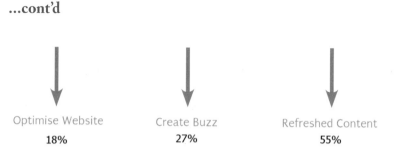

Optimise Website	Create Buzz	Refreshed Content
18%	27%	55%

If Google ranking is important to you, then you need those little spiders to come back to your website as often as possible, so please feed them as much information as you can.

As mentioned previously, Google likes new content on your website, but it gives more weight (or favoritism) to certain types of content. These are split into branded and unbranded content.

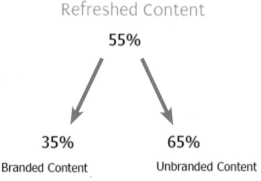

Refreshed Content

55%

35% | 65%

Branded Content | Unbranded Content

Branded content

Branded content simply means any pages on your website that are talking about your company. Good examples are the "About us" section, "Meet the team", "Features and benefits of your products or services", "Contact us" page or even a testimonial page. These pages are known as "branded content" and it is important to change and update these pages as regularly as possible, but it does not have as much impact on the Google algorithm as "unbranded content".

Unbranded content

Unbranded content is content that has the visitor in mind rather than your business. Google favors content that your visitors find interesting and helpful. Examples of good "unbranded content" are:

- Frequently asked questions page
- Toolkit
- Blogs/news or articles that are about your industry and relevant to your audience (not blogs about your new employee, or how you have raised lots of money in a charity event that you did at the weekend)

If you do have a blog or a news feature on your website then we recommend adding an article as an absolute minimum at least once every two weeks (300-700 words). The more content you create, the better your chances are of being indexed.

Make sure that the content you are posting is relevant to your industry, sector, product or business. If you constantly provide irrelevant content then this will have a negative effect on your social media.

> **Do you regularly update the content on your website to keep the Google spiders happy? If "yes", then give yourself a point.**

Data capture process

As any good marketer will tell you, email is probably the most powerful tool to talk directly to your audience. There were many blogs floating around the Internet a few years ago saying that email will soon be dead, and people will just communicate on social networking platforms. There will probably always be a place for email, as well as the telephone and even printed matter. Capturing those all important email addresses from your website visitors is a no-brainer, but so many people go about it in the wrong way.

The words "subscribe to our newsletter" can be considered as words of doom. People are so worried about spam and privacy nowadays, that they become reluctant to enter their email address into those types of forms.

Visitors to your site will donate their email address to you if they feel that they are getting something in return. A free eBook, or a special offer, a discount coupon, techniques on a specific subject, the first chapter of a book, register for job alerts, legal updates, property searches… the list is endless. The important part is what you do with that email address once you have received it.

Beware

Avoid using the terminology "subscribe to our newsletter".

34

Do you have any means of capturing email addresses on the homepage of your website? If there is a data capture process that is buried within certain pages of your site then this does not earn you any points. You can only tick the box if this process is captured on the homepage.

Social sharing tools

Please do not confuse these with "social media links". Social sharing, or (otherwise known as social proof buttons), are a fantastic way for your content to be shared by your audience.

In this picture (from *SocialMediaExaminer.com*) they clearly display the power of a good social sharing tool. You can see that 1229 people have clicked on the Tweet button and shared this article onto their Twitter page, therefore driving more traffic back to their website.

This is a powerful tool and one not to be ignored. The key items that you should be adding a social sharing tool to are:

- Your blogs or news articles
- Your frequently asked questions page
- Your special offers or free downloads
- Your jobs (if a recruiter), or properties if an estate agent/realtor
- Your toolkit page

If you are a WordPress user, then you could try a fabulous plugin called **Alternate Digg Digg**. This is a floating toolbar (as seen in the example above), and will stay with your visitor as they read your article. It is much more effective than having a sharing tool at the top of your article, or at the bottom.

> **Do you have social sharing tools on your website? If you can answer "yes", then congratulations, you have another tick in the box!**

Don't forget

Remember, that Google loves it when people share your content, so make it easy for your visitors to do this.

Hot tip

If you only have social sharing tools for Facebook & Twitter, but your main target market is more business-to-business, then consider adding Google Plus and LinkedIn.

Social media links

Do you have social media icons on your homepage of your website?

It is also worth noting that usually there is no reason for a company to be present on ALL social networking platforms. It is important to have a presence on the social networking sites where your target market is talking.

Here is a list of social networking sites that are usually present on websites as clickable icons. Key social networking sites are discussed in more detail later in the book. However, if your target market is not active on a particular platform, then there is no point in wasting time, money and effort in trying to make it work. Spend that valuable time and money on platforms that work for you.

- Twitter
- Facebook
- LinkedIn
- Foursquare
- YouTube
- Google Plus
- Pinterest
- Instagram

If you have social media icons with links on your website then you cannot quite tick the box yet! Check to see that all the links go to the right places.

Check that all your social networking icons are directed to the correct site.

...cont'd

For example:

When you click on the Facebook icon, you will be redirected to the company Facebook page. Likewise, with Twitter and the YouTube account.

Double check that your icons are not social sharing tools as this often confuses your audience. Social sharing tools should not be visible in the header as it is on this example below.

Check that the link your LinkedIn icon goes to your **company** page, and not your **personal** profile.

These are social networking tools, NOT links to the social networking sites

| Home | Digital marketing | Workshops | Blog | Contact | Training | About | Tweet 1,068 | Like 0 | 8+1 24 |

If you have a LinkedIn icon, make sure that this is being redirected to the LinkedIn Company page and not a LinkedIn personal profile, unless you specifically wanted this option.

Do you have your social media links on the homepage of your website, and if so, do they redirect to all the right places? Then give yourself a point.

Is your site mobile friendly?

It's no secret that the mobile web is growing, and growing fast. It seems impossible to go out in public without seeing someone with a smartphone in his or her hand. What many may not realize is just how powerful the mobile web is actually becoming. With more and more people accessing the Internet from their mobile devices, websites that aren't optimized for mobile may become lost in the fold.

Did you know that mobile searches have grown 400% since 2010 and a survey concluded that 57% of people wouldn't recommend a business with a bad mobile site. *(Sources: Gartner, 2010; Google Internal Data, 2011; Cisco, 2011; Google "The Mobile Movement: Understanding Smartphone Users", 2011.)*

So, how do you know if your site is mobile friendly, apart from the obvious and looking at the site on your own smartphone or tablet?

Visit **http://snippets.hubspot.com/hubspot-device-lab** and test your website for free. This software displays your mobile phone on a variety of smartphones and tablets so you can see what your visitors will be viewing.

HubSpot's Device Lab

Sometimes it is not necessary to have a fully responsive website, but there are some key elements that you do need to consider:

- Can the text be easily read without scrolling, pinching or zooming?
- Can customers call you with a single press of a button?
- Are page links large enough to click with your thumb?
- If you are a retailer, is your store locator visible on the home screen?
- Does your website look professional and inviting to use?

> **Did your website pass the mobile friendly test? If so, then please allocate yourself a point in the checklist at the end of this chapter.**

Do you have a visible telephone number?

It is a well-known fact that the more visitors have to click within your site to find the information that they need, the more it dilutes that all-important conversion. You have probably visited websites in the past, and even on the Contact Us page there is no phone number, or sometimes not even an email address; there may only be a box to complete with details of your message. As a consumer, this is highly frustrating, when all you want is to talk to someone.

There was an interesting experiment taken by a company called TheFlowr.com, which can be found at this website: **http://blog. kissmetrics.com/results-from-flowr/**

Here is an extract from this experiment. The image below is the original Flowr homepage. If you look closely, you will see that there is no phone number on the page.

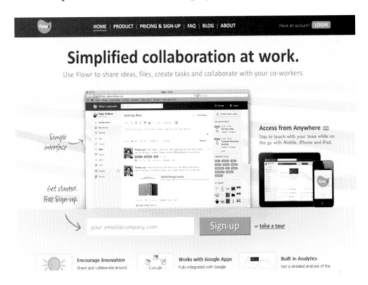

Hot tip

Having a telephone number visible in the header of your website is paramount for most small business owners. However, if you do include this in the header of your website, the phones should be managed during normal working hours as it's even more frustrating for customers if the phone isn't answered or they have to wait in a queue for a long time. If providing telephone support isn't viable, then it's best to put your contact number on the Contact Us page rather than your homepage.

In the next image, you will see a screenshot of the homepage variant, with a phone number and the call to action "Want to have a chat? Call us at…" (look for the red asterisk).

...cont'd

Flowr ran a simple A/B test with one homepage variation. Again, the only difference in the variation homepage was the addition of a small phone number and some supporting call-to-action text.

The results were as follows.

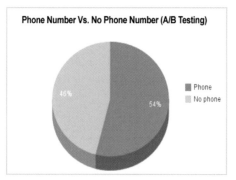

Davorin Gabrovec from Flowr concluded:

"Even though we didn't receive a lot of calls, I believe that having a phone number visible on the website gives more credibility to our product and trust to our visitors. When we re-design our website we will definitely include appropriate space for a bigger phone number."

Does your website have a visible telephone number on the homepage of your website? If "yes", then please allocate yourself a point in the checklist at the end of this chapter.

Testimonials and reviews

Nothing can make or break your company quicker than people talking. The fact is, we are human beings and people listen to what others say. It is probably more important than ever to make those words count.

Before you make the decision to skip this section because you are of the mindset "I do not want to add my clients onto my website for my competitors to find out who my clients are", then please take five minutes to read this section of the book.

We all know how fast bad news can travel. If someone is unhappy with your product or service, then they are more likely to talk about it. (See the Reputation Management section on pages 19-20).

If your business has 20 testimonials or positive reviews on its website, then this will far outweigh the one negative comment that people may say online about your business.

If your competitors are any good, then they will already know who your clients are. If a competitor views a testimonial on my website, I feel that the message I am sending out to those competitors is "I have this awesome relationship with this client, so beware competitors!"

Avoid "wet lettuce" testimonials. Here are examples of wet lettuce testimonials:

> "Very Positive! Staff are always helpful and obliging. Also you found me the exact job that I wanted in the location that I wanted."
> **Community Safety Officer**
>
> "In the 15 months I contracted I was placed five times and eventually into a permanent position. Excellent support. Always paid on time, never needed to doubt that I would be placed. Was always certain of a placement and therefore an income."
> **IT Support & Training Officer**

...cont'd

The website this is from had over 20 testimonials. However, there may be some doubt about the credibility of the content. Who is IT Support & Training Officer? Your website visitors will also be doubting your credibility if you have vague testimonials like this. Therefore, why would you highlight this on your website?

There are four main types of effective testimonials that should be displayed:

The video testimonial

Having a customer give a video testimonial is probably the most powerful of all testimonials as you can see the whites of their eyes and see how genuine they are. Adding a video testimonial onto YouTube and then streaming this into your own website is also an additional way of increasing your search engine optimization. Remember, Google owns YouTube.

Adding a visual along with a full name and company name

You can link your testimonial page to your LinkedIn personal profile, or your Google Plus Company Page, where you can collect reviews online. The reviews then can be displayed on your website in the format as below. This offers credibility. You are also offering additional credibility by adding a photo or a name with a hyperlink back to the individual's profile, indicating that they are genuine:

Glenn Wynsor – Director - Doodle-Doo Personalised Cards

With Social Media it's not just knowing about it, the value is in taking part in it and as much as it would be nice to do it all in-house the reality is that it generally just doesn't happen – however good the intention. So finding a great professional to manage it all for you is the very best alternative. That's why we are working with Green Umbrella on our new business, Doodle-Doo; we know it will make a difference.

Julie Edmondson – Recruitment Manager - Jobwise

I have attended 2 sessions run by Julia and she never ceases to inform and inspire me. Her enthusiasm knows no bounds; she is passionate about what she does and that shows in her delivery, her sessions are fun, informative and business critical – I've learned so much from her. Always on hand to help too if you need advice on any area of LinkedIn, Facebook or any other form of social media, highly recommended.

Audio testimonial

Adding a mini audio player of a recording of a positive testimonial is also exceptionally powerful. This can easily be achieved using some free software called **Audioboo**, or look at something called **Podbean**. Audioboo is also a neat little tool to interview your team and add the little snippets of information to your website.

Hot tip

Check out www. audioboo.com to record your audio testimonials and add them to your website. Easily accessible via an app on Android, iOS or Windows phone.

Social Mediators

Jenny Bardell – The Healthy One!

Jenny is an absolute treasure and has a wicked sense of humour. She also runs another business in her spare time, as well as having two boys at home – how she finds the time I will never know. She is officially super woman! Click play to find out if Jenny drinks red or white!

Juliadoherty
Jenny Bar...
audio♦Boo

Jane Pollard – The Book Lover!

Jane joined Green Umbrella to manage one particular client, and now she is running 4!. Jane's attention to detail certainly put's mine to shame, which is why she always ends up with the contracts that are a little more technical. She loves camping, anything to do with literacy and her favourite camping song is.....

Juliadoherty
Say hi to ...
audio♦Boo

Matt Heseltine – The Theatrical One!

Matt is an absolute delight to work with. He has a cheeky sense of humour, which is heightened by his strong Yorkshire accent. As well as running a variety of social media management clients for GUHQ, Matt also runs his own Theatre Company. He is a natural with the written word and producing content for our clients comes easy to him. Have a listen to his audio and his sense of humour comes across loud and clear!

Juliadoherty
Matt Hesl...
audio♦Boo

Case studies

Having a full case study, or completed portfolio, is also very powerful on your website. The more detail the better.

Adding a testimonial/review or case study to your website helps to give your potential clients confidence that you are worth doing business with. Feeling comfortable with you, your product and your professionalism is often the main reason why people will, or will not, do business with you.

...cont'd

Case studies work extremely well if you have a before/after scenario such as this website for Butterworth Cox.

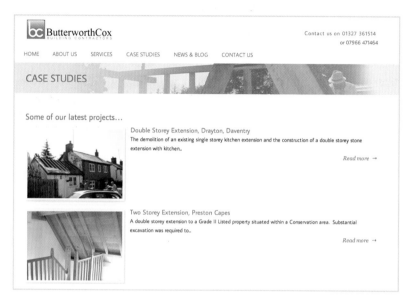

Do you have credible testimonials or reviews on your website? If "yes", then give yourself a point in the checklist at the end of this chapter.

Do you offer a guarantee?

Today's new generation of bloggers and entrepreneurs have discovered that having a guarantee, an age-old offline technique, can be one of the most powerful routes to more sales.

They know that online buyers are plagued by fears and doubts. And there's nothing that will kill a sale faster than doubt.

"But putting a guarantee on my website can be a high risk", I hear you think aloud. This is so not true and is a complete misconception.

So what makes a good guarantee? Here are some ideas for you:

Look at your competitors
What are they guaranteeing to their customers?

Look at your strengths
What area of your business do you excel in? Do you do fast installations? Do you respond quickly to a customer? Do you have the widest selection in town? Do you save money for your customers?

Guarantee results
This could be delivery times, what good things happen when customers use your products? Better relationships? More money? Reduced stress? Write down the answer in specific detail, and then guarantee that outcome. (Just make sure you can fulfill on your promise.)

Choose a payback
Remember only a small volume of customers will ever take you up on a payback. You want to create an attractive payback in case customers are unsatisfied. Ideally, it won't cost you much but will have a high-perceived value. A hassle-free, money-back guarantee is a good place to start. But try to dress it up a bit. Remember, a better-than-risk-free best guarantee is the best guarantee of all. Yours should exceed customer expectations and be memorable.

Having numerous guarantees on your site to instil confidence in the various products and services that you provide will enhance the possibility of those all-important sales conversions.

> **Do you have a guarantee on your website? If so, then please award yourself a point in the checklist at the end of this chapter.**

Remember, your potential buyers feel a certain level of risk whenever you offer something to them. A guarantee is your best tool for lowering or eliminating that risk.

45

Important and legal information

If your business is a registered limited company in the UK, for instance, then it is a legal requirement to display your company details. You are required to add the following on your website: your company's registered name; place of registration; company registration number, and registered office address.

This could be added as a footnote to your homepage, an addition on the Contact us or About us page, or within your terms of business.

Hot tip

Check out the legal requirements for your own country. For instance:

UK: http://companieshouse.gov.uk/promotional/busStationery.shtml

US: http://legalzoom.com

Canada: http://www.canadabusiness.ca/eng/page/2764/

Australia: http://legal123.com/au/

If your website collects user data (i.e. you may have a Contact Us form, or an opt-in form where people need to leave their email address) you must display a privacy policy informing the user what the business does with the data and that it conforms to the Data Protection Act.

If you are using Google Analytics (see pages 258-260, or other visitor analysis packages, or any type of CMS (Content Management System), the law in the UK requires you to retrieve consent from your visitors that it is OK for you to monitor and record their activity on your site, and a whole bunch of other information. Just having a small note about how you use cookies in your terms of business is not acceptable. You need a cookie policy pop-up that is visible immediately to the visitor as soon as they land on your website. This website is very helpful: **http://www.seqlegal.com/**

Check online before implementing any new procedures on your site, as these rules often change.

Beware

If you are requesting visitors to surrender their personal details, then make sure you have a privacy policy on your website.

Don't forget

If your website is collecting cookies, it is a legal requirement in the UK to have a pop-up cookie policy.

Conclusion

The four steps to online marketing success:

Build your platform
Hopefully you scored high in the 10 steps described in this chapter, which means that you have achieved step one for building your website.

Grow your network
If you have implemented a data capture process, added numerous pages which are "unbranded content", and consistently drip feed your audience with good blogs, articles, news or events then you have achieved step two – grow your network.

Define a listening, engagement and content strategy
Have you activated comments in your news? Have you put together a marketing plan for your content on your site? Have you set up a listening strategy, and registered with **mention.net**? If so, then you have achieved step three – define a strategy.

Measure the results
Have you got Google Analytics on your site? Have you set your Google Analytics goals? Are you looking at your statistics? Do you know where your traffic is coming from? What is your bounce rate? How many unique visitors do you have to your site each week? Is this increasing? Do you know where you are ranked in Google? If you have the answers to all these questions and you are regularly monitoring and tweaking your site to improve its performance, then you have accomplished step four and you are on your way to website marketing success.

Checklist

How did you score on the 10-point checklist for your website?

1 Do you have "Calls to Action" on your homepage?

2 Is your "We to You" ratio healthy?

3 Are you adding new content to your website on a regular basis?

4 Do you have a data capture process?

5 Are there social sharing tools on your site?

6 Do you have social media links on the homepage of your website and do they go to the right place?

7 Is your site mobile friendly?

8 Do you have a visible contact number in the header?

9 Do you have credible testimonials, case studies or reviews on your website?

10 Do you offer a guarantee?

3 Blogging

What is a blog?

A blog is short for "web-log". A blog was originally created for people who like to produce journals, and therefore those who traveled and wanted to record their adventures would be seen as a blogger. Things have moved on since those early days, and a blog is so much more, nowadays. Here is the official definition of a blog:

blog

/bläg/ ◄))

noun

1. a personal website or web page on which an individual records opinions, links to other sites, etc. on a regular basis.

verb

1. add new material to or regularly update a blog.
   "it's about a week since I last blogged"

What are the main differences between a blog and a regular website?

- Blogs are usually updated frequently, sometimes multiple times a day.

- When a website is changed, that information is gone forever. However, with a blog the information stays online in chronological order.

- Blogs are easy to maintain. However, a website blogger may need an understanding of coding, and other web skills.

- Blogs are used for communication, and they encourage people to join in discussions on a topic.

- There are whole communities of bloggers for specific industries, and this world is vibrant.

- Blogging gives you an instant way to publish your thoughts, opinions and ideas online.

The term "blog" was not coined until the late 1990s, which is when the Internet really started to take off. When you analyze all of the points on the opposite page and then look at the key factors that Google uses for search engine ranking (mainly refreshed content), you can see why blogging from a business perspective has been a positive step in the right direction.

Why is blogging important?

Blogging is important for all businesses. Whether you are a micro, small or multinational organization, blogging should be integral to your online content marketing strategy. Here are the four main reasons that you should be blogging for your business:

Drive traffic to your website

Your blog gives you a platform to create relevant content for your clients and prospects. If used as a marketing tactic to drive traffic to your website it can be extremely powerful.

If driving traffic back to your website is a key strategy for your business (see pages 17-18), then make sure that your blog is either built into your website, or is embedded in your website. If the blog is elsewhere online, then you may be providing valuable information that will attract traffic to your blog, not your website. Therefore, those visitors will not have the opportunity to explore your website, or be attracted by one of your calls to action.

If your business is active on social networking sites such as Facebook, Twitter, Pinterest, LinkedIn or Google Plus, then posting your article title (with an image) and a link so that potential readers can click to read the full article, and drive more traffic back to your site is strongly recommended.

Here is a typical blog post on Facebook, which will drive traffic back to Michael Hyatt's website:

Link to Michael's blog article

Hot tip

You can also use an excerpt when posting your blog. An excerpt is a "read more" link. So viewers receive a teaser in their email, but need to click to view the full article on your website.

Sorry Could You Say That Again? - The Benefit Of Video As A Social Tool

The chances are that if you are interested in this blog you probably business, or you work for a company that want's you to reach out t When you come right down to it - that is the lifeblood of all busine out to people and basically we go..

Continue Reading...

Beware

Try not to manipulate the system by adding keywords where they are not appropriate. Your key focus should be on the user experience, not on how Google works.

...cont'd

Another way to attract traffic to your website using your blog is to utilize email. As mentioned in the previous chapter, it is important to capture those all important email addresses from your website. Once captured, they can be stored on any type of email marketing software such as MailChimp, Constant Contact, Infusionsoft or something similar. Ask your web developers to set up an RSS campaign (see page 70) to feed your blog to all those that have subscribed or given you their email address.

Increase your search engine optimization

As mentioned in the previous section, having regular fresh content that is unique and not regurgitated content is now the biggest influence for Google ranking. The easiest way to achieve new content to your website is to add a blog and then make regular contributions.

Use keywords in your articles. List the keywords, topics, and categories you want your business to be found with. Use these words, and related expressions, when writing your posts.

Of course, whether you actively seek these out or not, blogging regularly about your business, industry, product or customer lifestyle will naturally increase your search keywords.

Keywords and topics on your website are a significant way in which Google (and other search engines) find your site for these searched words.

Position your brand as an industry leader

Quality written articles demonstrate you or your company as a thought leader in your industry. By posting relevant topics about your industry or sector you will also provide "under the radar selling" which means you can easily bring your products and services into the article in a subtle way, as a solution to the topic that you are writing about.

If you are a retailer, for example, write blog posts about your products. Your customers will get to know you as the knowledge source for the products they want.

If you are in business-to-business, then post articulate, well researched articles about your service industry. Become the place to be for your niche market.

Develop better customer relationships

Blogs provide another source to deepen the connection with your customer. By connecting directly on your website, your clients are able to get to know your business or product from the comfort of their computer, smartphone or tablet. Use this. Again, build trust by being a source of information. Consumers like to be informed, and appreciate that you are the one teaching them.

Unlike many social sites, a blog is generally searchable on your site for a long time. Your website comments last longer than a Twitter response or Facebook post. Other customers will see your interactions too. It is important that you respond, though. If someone posts a comment on your blog, then make sure that you are responding to that comment within a few hours. You want people to feel that you are listening to them, and that you value their contribution.

We recommend a plugin called **http://disqus.com/** for WordPress site to achieve this. Disqus software has a whole community of its own which is great for stimulating additional interaction and engagement on your website.

As mentioned, a real sin of social media and blogging is to post your blog, then have lots of comments, without responding or getting involved. Ensure that you have your notifications set on, and that you have some type of spamgate that will sift out all the robots that spam your site.

There are many spammers out there and if your website is open, then it is highly probable that they will start leaving random comments on your blog. To spot a spammer, look out for the following:

- They usually start with a compliment of your website or blog, but they never refer to anything specific. For example: "What awesome content! Thank you for providing this great blog."
- The spelling and grammar is usually awful.
- They will always have a link to somewhere in the post.
- Sometimes, they will simply try to sell something, in a similar way to which you receive spam emails.

Place these in the trash, and then signify them as junk, in the same way you would on email.

You are building trust, too. The more you can show that you are well-versed in your field, the more likely your potential customer will trust you to supply what they need.

Do not regurgitate other people's content. Write unique content at all times.

Where to host your blog

There are many popular blogging platforms that you can use. As previously mentioned, it is best to have your blog incorporated into your main website. Alternatively, your blog could be your main website, using a well-known platform called WordPress. Alternative platforms are those such as Tumblr, Typepad, Blogger, etc. But WordPress is by far the most superior, as explained in this infographic by **www.100webhosting.com**

WordPress is not just a blogging platform; it is a complete content management system (CMS) that you can build your whole site on, which obviously incorporates a blog. The In Easy Steps website (**ineasysteps. com**) is a WordPress-built site.

Indeed, some of the most famous websites are also built on WordPress. If WordPress is good enough for the Rolling Stones, then it should be good enough for your business, too!

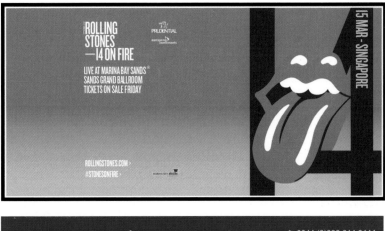

There are two types of WordPress CMS systems. See pages 56-57 to ensure you're using the correct platform.

Some other top sites based on WordPress that you may not be aware of are:

- Forbes – **http://www.forbes.com**
- SAP – **http://en.sap.info/**
- Usain Bolt, the world's fastest man – **http://usainbolt.com/**
- Katy Perry – **http://www.katyperry.com/**

If you are considering using WordPress, then please be aware that there are two types: WordPress.com and WordPress.org. This can be confusing, so we'll show you the pros and cons of each.

...cont'd

There are two main differences between the two sites:

Cost

WordPress.com – it's a free service, and you will have a website address that looks like: "joebloggswebsite.wordpress.com" (this is the same if you are using other free services such as blogger).

WordPress.org – it is chargeable, and you will have a website address that looks more like: "joebloggs.co.uk" or "joebloggs.com" (there is no mention of WordPress at all, and this is much more professional if you are running a business).

Flexibilty

WordPress.com – you are limited to how you can design the site, and the functionality that you can bring to the site.

WordPress.org – you can integrate the site with your email marketing software such as MailChimp or AWeber, as well as many other applications to make your site funky and marketable.

Sometimes "free" is not always best. You may think that starting out with a WordPress.com site is a good way to begin, but I would advise jumping in at the deep end, getting yourself a WordPress.org self-hosted site with a professional address (domain name), and go for it.

Summary of differences:

	WordPress.ORG	WordPress.COM
Is it free?	You can download it for free. However, you will need a domain and hosting which will incur a cost. (Usually a low cost monthly figure).	The basic package is free. But there is a premium package available if you need additional storage.

	WordPress.ORG	WordPress.COM
Set up time	Approximately 15 minutes	Approximately 5 minutes
What about plugins and applications?	There are lots, and lots, and lots! At the time of writing this book there were 29,372 plugins, increasing all the time!	20-30 plugins that are only accessible for premium users.
Can I monetize my site?	If you want, you can monetize your blog and add different adverts. You have complete control and decide which ads go where and how many you would like.	You are not able to add or sell any kind of adverts unless you receive over 25,000 page views a month.
Updates and maintenance	Updating the blog is your responsibility. It is also highly recommended that you do backups as often as possible. However, updates take a few seconds to complete, and there are plugins to help with backing up your site automatically.	No need to worry. WordPress.com is responsible for your updates and backups.
Storage	Depends on your hosting company. Usually unlimited.	3GB for free (see tip)

Don't forget

You cannot upload video files, audio files, zip files or music without the WordPress.com Premium package (which includes 10GB extra storage), or the Business plan (which includes unlimited storage):

Premium plan: http://store.wordpress.com/plans/premium/

Business plan: http://store.wordpress.com/plans/business/

Abide by the 80/20 rule and you can't go wrong.

Hot tip

Use questions often in your daily posts.

Writing the blog post

You have set up your blog, but now what? What on earth do you write about?

One common mistake is people constantly writing about themselves, and what is happening in their business. This is interesting on occasions, but not constantly.

If you are aware of the Pareto Principle (or the 80/20 rule) then the same theory applies to blogging.

80% of your business comes from 20% of your efforts

Therefore 20% of your blog posts should be something to do with your company, your products or services. However, 80% of your posts should incorporate information to do with your industry. They should be topics that are of interest to your visitors.

Some good hooks for you are

Questions that you are often asked on email or on the phone. If someone calls and says, "How do you…?", or "I am after some advice, what do you think…?", note these questions down; they will make excellent blog topics.

Your industry will have trade magazines, or press articles that will give you some fantastic content ideas for a good blog.

Check out LinkedIn Pulse (see page 197) – once you have customized your news, you will find lots of topics of interest that you can easily blog about.

LinkedIn Pulse has some great content ideas for your blog

All Updates ▾

Pulse recommends this news for you

Why I Won't Be Deactivating My Facebook Account Anytime Soon
Patrick Boylan on LinkedIn · It seems like there is now a trend among some social media "experts" [substitute with "hipsters" if you like] is to…
6h

The Wheel of Fortune
By Christian Myong Choi · 1h

Why 33% of College Grads Are Regretful
By Jennifer Lee · 1d

Another way to produce consistent content is to choose a theme for the month, and focus on topics within that theme. You can then plan content for the forthcoming four weeks, or even the whole year.

If you have a small team of people then look at some software such as Passle (**http://home.passle.net/**), which is a fantastic tool that lets you and your team collate ideas for future blogs.

How does Passle work?
Once you have registered an account with Passle, you have a choice of adding a bookmark, or a Google Chrome extension to your browser.

When you see an article online that you consider a worthy topic for your own blog, simply highlight the text within the blog so it turns blue, and then click the Passle icon.

It is a quick and easy way to collect ideas for blogs with the touch of a button when you are surfing online. You can access your ideas at any time, and there is an option to add team members, who can also add their ideas for blogs onto your account, ensuring that you will never hit a dry spell for content creation for your site.

Consider choosing a theme for your updates for a set time period.

Using Passle is a fabulous way of collecting your blogging ideas.

...cont'd

Do not get distracted

When you are writing a blog article it is important to block out distractions. Turn off your email notifications; make sure that you do not have your social networking notifications on. Being disciplined can be very difficult to do, but there is an answer to this dilemma in the form of the software called Anti-Social (**www.anti-social.cc**).

Anti-social is brilliant! Simply add your relevant social networking sites, or any other website that you may be tempted to view that will distract you. You could add Google Analytics, your website, Hootsuite as well as the regular social networking sites.

Once you have added your social networking sites, you click the little icon on your desktop and set the time for how long you would like to be offline. In the screenshot below, you can see that I have set my time for 120 minutes, which is how long I usually take to write and record a new blog post. I then decide if I want to have access to my emails or not.

You've set Anti-Social to be offline for 120 minutes.

If you need access to email and chat, select Email Access. If not, select Normal Mode.

After selecting a mode, Anti-Social will ask for your password. Anti-Social requires administrator access.

Cancel   Email Access   Normal Mode

Now the magic happens. If I try to access one of the websites that I may be tempted to view, I receive a message saying "Unable to access the network".

So all I need to do is turn off the software right? Wrong! To cancel the application I need to reboot my computer. I find that it is a fabulous tool and has kept me focused on my goal for writing blog articles on a regular basis. There is a small charge for the software, but if you find that you are easily distracted then it is certainly worth the investment.

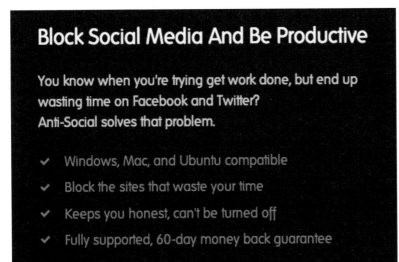

Being active on social media can be very disruptive to your work flow. If you are easily distracted then consider downloading "Anti-Social" software.

Have you included a visual within your blog article?

Is there a process to blogging?

Blogging is an art, and it is important that you have some consistency in the way your blogs look and feel. To make it easy for you, here is a simple checklist for the steps needed to operate a successful blog.

1 Write the blog post

- Does the content show personality and is it conversational?
- Will the readers get value from the article (make sure it is not salesy)?
- Does it answer a question, issue or other topic your readers need or want to know?
- Have you included some type of fact, figure or statistic?
- Use spell checker.
- Read the article out loud. This is very important, as it is the easiest way to pick up mistakes.
- Ask another person to proofread the article for spelling and grammar.

2 Format your blog post on the website

- Is it easy on the eye? Lists and short paragraphs work really well.
- Headlines from the content – a book called "Advertising headlines that make you rich" by David Garfinkle, has some great ideas.
- Bullets for lists – makes it easy reading for visitors.

3 Tag and hyperlink external and internal sources to further explain points made

To turn a word blue, so that your audience knows that they can click on the word and it will be directed to a website, simply highlight the word with your mouse, and then click "Ctrl + K" on a PC or "cmd + K" if on a Mac.

Insert Hyperlink

Link to: Paste your website address here...

Display: wordpress

ScreenTip...

Web Page | Document | E-mail Address

Recent Addresses ▸   Launch E-mail Application

To:

Subject:

Enter the e-mail address and subject for messages that will be created when people click on this link.

Cancel   OK

If you are writing your article on WordPress or within an online platform, then look for the hyperlink icon. Then add your website address.

Highlight your word, then click this link icon

B *I* ABE ≡ ≡ 66 — ≡ ≡ ≡ 🔗 — ≡ ⌨ 🐦 🛒 ▾

Paragraph ▾ U ≡ A ▾ 📋 ⊘ Ω ≡ ≡ ↶ ↷ ❓

4 **Add an image – with a title and an alt description**

It is imperative that you are using a copyright-free image, or an image that you have the rights to use. There are numerous places where you can obtain images.

A number of stock images can be found on these sites. However, this is not an exhaustive list:

http://www.dreamstime.com/ – this is the site that we use most often. However, it is a personal choice. Dreamstime offers a range of free images that you can use within your blog, but the best images come with a cost.

http://www.gettyimages.co.uk/ – Getty Images allow you to use any of their images that has the embed facility within your blog, or on social networking platforms, as long as you are not using the image to promote a product or service for commercial use. They do have certain rules

Don't forget

See page 68 for more on alt description.

...cont'd

Beware

Be aware of copyright legislation, and ensure all of the images within your website are legal.

that you need to abide by. See: **http://www.gettyimages. co.uk/Corporate/Terms.aspx**

http://www.istockphoto.com/

http://www.thinkstockphotos.co.uk/

http://www.photos.com/

http://www.shutterstock.com/

5 **Add a call to action, or an affiliated image**

Make the most of each article that you produce by adding a strong call to action. This can be a simple question that you ask – for example:

"Do you have an opinion on XXXX? Please comment in the box below."

Or another option is to have a range of banner adverts designed so that you can change them depending on the content of the blog. Here is a selection of banner adverts that we add at the end of each article:

Once you have added your image, then hyperlink the image (using the same technique as previously mentioned) to the area on your website that gives more detail about the product or service.

6   Add a minimum of four related articles

A little bit like some online stores: you bought this; you may also be interested in these products...

Hot tip

Add related articles to the bottom of each blog article to ensure a good user experience.

As well as a call to action, add related articles to the bottom of your blog posts so they look like this:

How did you do on your website? Did you get 5/5? I would love to hear from you.
Please feel free to comment below.

Web Design
Is your website working for you?

For a FREE Health Check
on your website click
HERE

Add strong calls to action

Related articles

- A Grave Message (green-umbrella.biz)
- 17 Social Media Books That Will Make You a Smarter Marketer (socialmediaexaminer.com)
- The Complete Checklist for Creating Compelling Calls-to-Action (hubspot.com)
- The smell of the audience, the roar of the greasepaint (green-umbrella.biz)
- 5 Design Tips to Boost Blog Conversions (mashable.com)

Add related articles

Make sure that at least one of these articles is linked back to a previous article within your OWN website. Google gives you extra points if visitors click within your site, so give them the opportunity to explore.

If you are a WordPress user, then consider using a plugin called Zemanta: **http://www.zemanta.com/**
Zemanta makes the whole process easy for you by the click of a button.

Zemanta offers these services as part of the plugin, which is currently free of charge.

7   SEO (search engine optimize) your blog post

By now, you can see why it takes approximately 1-2 hours to create and edit a blog post, but it is worth the investment of time to get it right.

If you are not an SEO expert, it is much easier to add a

...cont'd

plugin to your website to ensure that you have ticked all the right boxes for optimizing your website for Google etc., than it is to learn the ins and outs of the fast changing world of search engine optimization.

There are lots of plugins out there, but Yoast **(https://yoast.com/WordPress/plugins/seo/)** is a plugin that is updated regularly, and is really easy to use with its green tick process.

To see if a plugin is a good one or not, check out how many downloads they have on the developer's site, along with the star rating. Here are the statistics for Yoast (*at the time of going to print*):

Image source: https://yoast.com/wordpress.plugins/seo/

...cont'd

Here is the checklist for a search engine optimization:

- Title has keyword.
- H tag with the keyword (H tag is a title, i.e. Heading 2, Heading 3 etc.).

Google likes tags. Select H2 or H3 tags for your blog headings/subheadings

- Keyword bolded in content.
- Keyword in the URL/website address (and the URL short and easy to decipher from other content). You can edit the Permalink, which changes the URL, but does not change the title of the article.

- Appropriate tags.
- Meta keyword – usually 1 or 2.
- Meta description – the Meta description is the area that you see in Google that describes the article. This area is a maximum of 156 characters in length. If you install a plugin such as Yoast, it is relatively easy to change the Meta description by completing a form.

...cont'd

Your LinkedIn 5 a day, are you doing yours? - Green Umbr...
www.green-umbrella.biz/2013/02/linkedin-5-day-yours/ ▾
20 Feb 2013 - **LinkedIn** is no exception, and each day we go through a process called the "**Linkedin 5 a day**". There are the five key activities that we perform ...

This is your meta description

- Picture Alt Tag with the keyword – an "alt tag" or "alternative tag" or sometimes called "alternative description" is a string of words that describes an image on a website. If you hover over an image, then you should see a "pop-up" of a word that has been alt tagged.

  So why use alt tags for your images? The simple answer is that Google can read text, but it cannot read images. Therefore, if you have not alt tagged your images, then Google will see lots of black holes within your website or blog. The other main reason for adding a second title or alternate description is to assist those who are visually impaired. If a user has the Accessibility function enabled on their computer, then when you hover over a tagged image, the computer will read the description out loud.

Don't forget

Make sure you have optimized your blog post for search engines.

Caption	How to block someone on LinkedIn
Alternative Text	How to block someone on LinkedIn

8 **Publish and distribute your post**

If you are feeling creative, then you may want to write a number of posts in one day and then schedule them throughout the week or month. Most blogging platforms will have a scheduling facility.

The process for distribution of blog is an automated process. Those who have subscribed to the blog receive new blogs into their inbox at the set time. **MailChimp** is an excellent tool for publishing and distributing posts. (See data capture process on page 34.)

Using evergreen content to republish

If at all possible, try to make some of the content on your blog "evergreen". This simply means that it is not date or time sensitive, so that you can publicize the content more than once on your different social networking sites.

In the early days of Green Umbrella, I would write a blog post for "What is new in social media this week", along with a video that I had created. Not only was it very time consuming to source the information needed, it also took about 3-4 hours to write the content, put the video together, upload to YouTube and then embed into my website. The content always had lots of hits, but it only had a lifeline of about two weeks and then it became irrelevant.

I learned the hard way, and I now try to only publish content that is evergreen. I keep the "What's new in social media" videos for my monthly coaching clients.

What is an RSS?

RSS is an abbreviation of Rich Site Summary, although most people now know it as Real Simple Syndication. This makes me chuckle as, in my opinion, RSS is far from simple.

The easiest way to describe the functionality of an RSS is to relate it to a magazine subscription. For example, if you have subscribed to receive a Camping magazine, then once a month the magazine will pop through your letterbox. An RSS is exactly the same but in the digital world. If you subscribe to an RSS for a website, then each time that website produces new content, the article will appear in your inbox, rather than relying on your memory to check the site to see if there is any new content.

RSS - Rich Site Summary

Filename extension	.rss, .xml
Internet media type	application/rss+xml (registration not finished)[1]
Type of format	Web syndication
Extended from	XML

Image source: Wikipedia

Hot tip

Do not register your article on any directories immediately. Wait a few days to allow Google to index your article on your own website first.

If you do not have any automated systems set up, here is a checklist of how to distribute your blog:

- Publish your blog on all of your social networks.
- Send an email to your contacts with a link to your blog.
- Register your articles on article directories such as:
  http://goarticles.com/
  http://ezinearticles.com/
  http://www.articlesbase.com/

Guest writers on your blog

There are benefits to being a guest writer on another website, but there are also some excellent benefits for having a number of regular guest bloggers on your own blog. Here are five reasons why you should consider having a guest blogger on a website:

Keeping your blog active

Unless you have a big team, it is very difficult to keep up with content on a regular basis. Consistent frequency is the key to any marketing strategy and blogging is no different. If you produce an article a week for a month, and then produce zero for the next month, then you will have a negative impact on your search engine results, and your audience will not know when to expect information from you. More people are likely to unsubscribe to your blog if you are not consistent. Having regular guest bloggers on your site is a great way to keep consistent in the frequency.

Build relationships

As with writing for other blogs, allowing guest posts on your own blog opens the door to building relationships with others in your industry. Networking is almost always a good thing, and it might just lead to profitable joint ventures down the road, you never know!

Increase traffic

If your guest blogger has a fan base, more than likely they'll come along for the ride when their article is published on your blog. The result is more traffic for your blog, and more exposure for you and your business. In addition, you could suggest that your guest blogger actually records them reading the article, which you can then produce as an audio blog. You will be surprised how many people are up for this challenge, and how much they will share the content with their own audience if they can also hear themselves, rather than just reading an article.

More content variety

With guest posts, you'll inject your blog with a bit of variety, which most of your readers will welcome. Different authors mean different topics, different perspectives, and different writing styles, all of which can keep your blog from becoming predictable and stale.

Increase guest blogging opportunities for you

Guest writers may return the favour and ask you to guest post on their blog. Take them up on their offer. You can benefit from the wider audience, increased traffic and a boost in reputation.

Ask others to guest blog on your website. Make sure that the content is unique by checking the content on **Grammerly. com**

Set some rules for your bloggers so it is clear what is expected from them.

Record an audio version of each blog article to help increase your traffic.

Conclusion

The four steps to online marketing success for blogging:

1 **Build your platform**

Have you built your blog correctly? Do you have keywords in your articles; is it optimized for search engines? Are you adding images and calls to action to your articles?

If your site is looking good, and indexed correctly, with regular content, then you have reached stage one of success for blogging.

2 **Grow your network**

Are your comments active? Do you have regular visitors? Do you have those all-important social sharing tools, which will help grow your network? Do you have guest bloggers contributing to your site?

If you are growing your network then congratulations, you are achieving the second stage of blogging success.

3 **Create your strategy**

Have you decided on how many posts to create each week/month? We recommend at least once every two weeks, keeping the Google spiders happy. Are you consistently producing articles? Are your response times quick on your blogging comments? Have you got a strategy for word count? Have you got a strategy for content topics? Have you set rules for your guest bloggers and given them allocated dates for them to send you content? Have you got a bank of calls to action ready to add to the bottom of your articles?

If you can answer yes to most of these questions, then you have accomplished stage three of your blogging success.

4 **Measure the results**

When it comes to measuring the results for your blog, you first need to see if your articles are pulling in traffic to your website. This can be achieved by looking at your Google Analytics (covered in pages 258-260).

Other measurements are recording how many people are actually sharing your articles to their network along with the volume of comments that you may (or may not) be receiving online on the various social networking channels and on the blog itself. I would highly recommend a tool called **https://sumall.com**, which gives an analysis once a day of all of your online platforms and is a handy tool to have.

If you are measuring the results, and tweaking your strategies to better those results, then congratulations! You are now a fully-fledged blogger.

Checklist

How did you score on the 10-point checklist for your blog?

1   Do you have a unique URL/website address for each blog?

2   Are visitors able to leave a comment on your blog?

3   Are your blog articles more than 300 words?

4   Do you have a visual (video or image) within each article?

5   Are your visitors able to easily share your content with their audience? (i.e. Do you have social media sharing tools incorporated within the blog?)

6   Do you have a call to action at the end of your articles?

7   Have you added "related articles" at the end of your blog to encourage readers to explore your site?

8   Have you optimized your blog post for Google? i.e. Included a meta description, added tags and links within the article?

9   Is ALL of your blog content original and unique? i.e. The content is not regurgitated from another website?

10   Are you producing evergreen content?

4 Facebook

An introduction to Facebook

Facebook is a fantastic marketing tool for many businesses, but it is not for everyone. The first question you need to ask yourself is "Do I need to be active on Facebook?". If your target market is not on Facebook, if this is not a platform where they are talking, then don't waste your time, effort and money here.

Don't forget

Facebook pages may vary, so the graphics that are showcased in this book may not look exactly the same as your Facebook page. Facebook is forever rolling out new features, and deleting old ones, so your page may not represent all of the features named in this book.

What are the demographics for Facebook?

As you can see, the biggest demographic on Facebook is 25-34 year olds, with 48% of these users checking their Facebook every day.

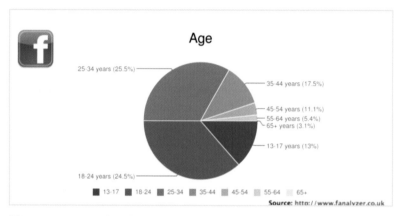

There is not much of a difference between a male and female split, which is nice to see.

Don't forget

48% of users check their Facebook every single day.

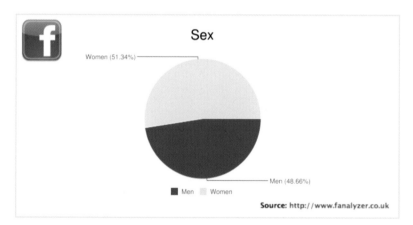

There is also an equal split in the demographics with regard to relationships; therefore, the biggest influence that we can take from these statistics is the age demographics, which perhaps does not help us much.

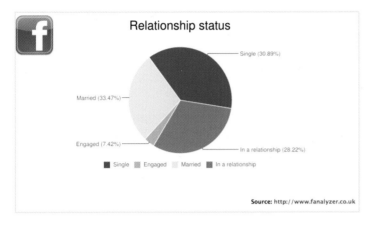

What industries thrive on Facebook?

Let us showcase some exceptionally good Facebook pages that were finalists in the **socialmediaexaminer.com** Top 10 Small Business Facebook Pages awards in 2012.

Recruit Military is a military-to-civilian recruiting firm, helping veterans and transitioning military service members and military spouses find civilian jobs, buy businesses and improve their education.

What the judges liked:

- Great use of images and quotes
- Love the way they are using Facebook events for their job fairs
- Clever use of "Find a Job Friday"
- Excellent combination of posts on military facts and resources

...cont'd

Earthegy is a retailer of ancient gems and modern jewelry.

What the judges liked:

- Cool use of shopping page
- Good fan engagement with photos
- Great use of discount promotion
- Lots of recommendations
- Rewards app is a smart way to get continual engagement

The Chicken Chick at Egg Carton Labels by ADozenGirlz is a retailer of chicken egg carton labels and other chicken-related products.

What the judges liked:

- The blog app is very well done
- Great niche site with tons of tips and images
- Fantastic engagement
- Good use of contents

- Good variety of posts demonstrating fun, chicken care, chicken crafts and personality

PoolSupplyWorld is an online retailer of parts and products for swimming pools and spas.

What the judges liked:

- Great timeline cover photo which is changed often
- Coupon option is well done
- Underwater camera giveaway aligns well with niche
- Good use of call to action in posts to spark engagement

If you have a pinch of creative flair and you are able to build a community, then Facebook will work for your business. From personal experience, there are a few industries that have failed on Facebook and these are mainly from the legal and financial industries.

Now it is your turn. Work through the rest of the chapter and see if you pass the 10-point checklist at the end of this chapter for your own Facebook page.

Create your Facebook account

Before you can create a Facebook business page, you must first create your personal Facebook account.

To create your personal account:

 Visit **www.facebook.com** and complete the online registration process.

 When you've finished the registration process you'll be sent an email. Click the link in the email to verify your account.

You won't be able to progress to set up a business page until you've verified your personal account.

To create your business page:

 Visit **www.facebook.com/pages**

 Follow the setup procedure, choosing your category carefully as this will decide your page features.

3 Complete all areas of your business page, as explained in the following pages of this chapter.

About

It cannot be stressed enough how important it is to have a completed "About" area on your Facebook page, so check to make sure that all areas are complete. There are always key areas that are often missed; therefore, we will walk you through these steps.

The first habit to develop when running a business page on Facebook is the function known as "switching". When you log into Facebook, you will automatically log in as your personal profile. If you are logging in as your Facebook page then you will need to link a personal profile to your page, otherwise some of the features that are mentioned in this book will not be available to you. These are highlighted as we go through each step.

"Switching" simply means clicking on the dropdown arrow, which is located to the right of your Facebook profile.

It is important to try to get used to Facebook language at this stage.

From here, you will see a menu, which takes you to your business page.

Once clicked, you will see that your name has now disappeared from the top and has been replaced with your business name.

Practice the art of "switching"

When you "switch" your personal name will disappear

It will be replaced with your company name. (You can switch back at any time)

...cont'd

 Once you have "switched" then you need to access the admin area – click **About**

Click here to access the admin area

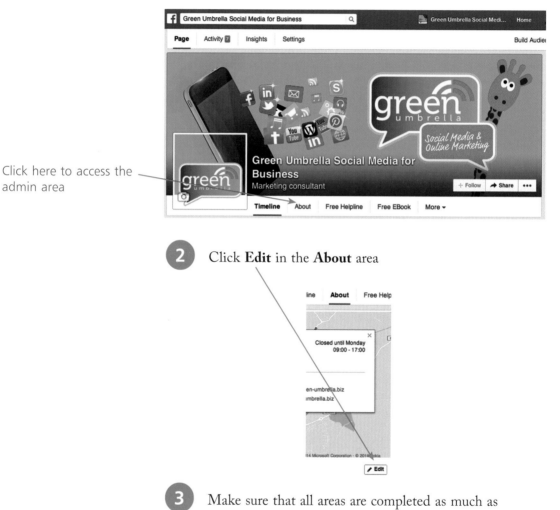

Click **Edit** in the **About** area

Make sure that all areas are completed as much as possible

Pay particular attention to these areas in the **Page Info** area:

Name – ensure that you have a keyword within your page name, which can be picked up in the Facebook search as well as Google searches. Please note that if your page has more than 200 likes then you are unable to change your name without contacting the Facebook support team, who will ask you for documents to support your request. This is discussed in more detail in on page 118.

Facebook web address – this is your unique URL, which is discussed in more detail on pages 84-85.

Your postal address – add your full postal address including the postcode/zip code.

Enter a short description and a long description as these appear in different places.

Also on – this links to sites such as Foursquare, Yelp, etc.

Do you have a fully completed "About us" area? If you can answer "yes" to this question then give yourself a point.

Grab your unique URL

When you register your company page on Facebook, you are allocated a URL (website address). However, the original URL is not very attractive and has a long stream of numbers after your page name like this:

🔒 https://**www.facebook.com**/pages/Salon-Alchemy/209205155771759

Having a URL that is easy to remember so that you can add it to your business cards, letterheads, and even tell to people that you meet is a real bonus. Therefore, you would like your Facebook URL (sometimes called a vanity URL or username) to look something like this:

🔒 https://**www.facebook.com**/outcasthairsalon

If you still have a URL for your page that has the long string of numbers after it, then follow these instructions to grab your unique URL for your Facebook page.

1 Log into Facebook, then visit **www.facebook.com/ username**
There is always more than one way to achieve the same results on Facebook, but this is probably the easiest way. Here you have options to edit two URLs:

Option 1 – The address for your personal Facebook profile
Option 2 – The address for your Facebook page

Remember a "profile" is a person and a "page" is a business.

84

Option 1

Option 2

Your page should be automatically selected from the dropdown menu.

2 Enter the username you want and click **Check availability**. You'll need to make sure that your username fits with Facebook guidelines (**https://www.facebook. com/help/105399436216001**).

Create your Facebook web address

Easily direct someone to your Page by setting a username for it. After you set your username, you may only change it once.

Page: | Green Umbrella Social Media for Business ⬍ |

Facebook web address | www.facebook.com/GreenUmbrellaBiz |

Green Umbrella Social Media for Business already has the username GreenUmbrellaBiz. You can visit it by going to http://www.facebook.com/GreenUmbrellaBiz. You may change this username once.

Check availability

Hot tip

Keep this username as short as possible.

Here are a few key things to remember before you click **Confirm**:

- You cannot claim a username that is already in use.
- Usernames are unique. Choose a username you'll be happy with for the long term. Usernames are not transferable, and you can only change your username once.
- Usernames can only contain alphanumeric characters (A-Z, 0-9) or a period (".").
- Periods (".") and capitalization don't count as a part of a username. For example, jonjones66, Jon.Jones66 and jon.jones.66 are all considered the same username.
- Usernames must be at least five characters long and can't contain generic terms.
- You must be Admin level to choose a username for a page.
- Make sure you're happy with your username (and double-check the spelling) before confirming it. Once you're sure you're happy, click "Confirm".

Hot tip

Your old URL will redirect to the new one, so you don't need to worry about updating your previous links.

Do you have your unique username? If "yes", then you are awarded another point on your checklist.

Branding your Facebook page

We have all heard the famous quote, "You never get a second chance to make a first impression". What is your current Facebook page saying about your business? There are three main areas in which you can brand your page:

The cover photo

This is your opportunity to show off your brand, and the cover photo is showcased loud and clear at the top of your page. This header-style image enables you to present your products, services and anything else that you wish to announce to the world. Facebook previously had very strict rules with regard to what you can and cannot add to a cover photo, but these were removed in 2013.

Currently, a cover photo is 851 pixels wide x 315 pixels deep. (Although these dimensions may change from time-to-time so it is always worth checking first).

Hot tip

Always add a description to your cover photos.

Cover photo

Update your cover photo at least once every two months to keep your page fresh. When you upload a new cover photo it is also posted on your timeline, giving your page greater visibility, so ensure that you always add a description, including a link to your website. Adding a description should not be ignored. Unfortunately, you cannot add a description at the same time as uploading a cover photo. Here is the process for changing and uploading a new cover photo.

 1 Hover over your cover photo with your mouse towards the bottom right hand corner. You will then see a prompt appear: **Change Cover**

Choose from the dropdown menu:

- **Choose From Photos** – this gives you the option to select from a previously uploaded cover photo
- **Upload photo** – this gives you the option to select an image from external sources
- **Reposition** – this gives you the option to edit your current cover photo
- **Remove** – if you click this option then you are left with a blank cover photo (not recommended)

For this exercise, let's explore the second option: Upload photo.

3 Select from your images the photo that you would like to upload. Remember, that it needs to be a minimum of 400 pixels wide. Double click your image

...cont'd

Double click your image

4 Use the **Drag to reposition cover** area until the image sits perfectly on your page, then click **Save Changes** when you are happy

5 Once you have saved the changes, then you need to add a description (this is the magic ingredient that helps with Google search, and will also encourage people to comment on your new cover photo). Click anywhere on the cover photo to access the area where you can add your description

Hot tip

A professionally designed cover photo can do wonders for your brand, and you can use them every year, so you only need them designed once.

Adding as much detail as you can, including a link to a specific product or service is ideal. Once you have completed this area in full, click **Finished editing** and you are good to go.

Hot tip

Change your cover photo at least once every two months.

Why not try some themes for your cover photos? Here are some examples of other themes that work well throughout the year:

- New Year
- Shrove Tuesday (Pancake Day)
- St Patrick's Day
- Mothering Sunday
- April Fools' Day
- Tennis, Grand Prix, Cricket & other major sporting events
- Thanksgiving
- International Day of Charity, Comic Relief, Sports Relief and other charity events
- Father's Day
- Summer time
- Back to School
- Bonfire Night
- Halloween
- Christmas

Plan your cover photo designs throughout the year.

...cont'd

The avatar/profile picture

Before we start, let's have a look at the Facebook guidelines for creating your profile picture.

"Page profile pictures are square and display at 160×160 pixels on your page. The photo you upload must be at least 180×180 pixels. We recommend uploading a square image. Rectangular images will be cropped to fit a square. Your page's profile picture will also display next to your page's name around Facebook to represent your page."

In my opinion, the avatar or profile picture is probably the most important image on your page, because it appears in so many places as well as next to your cover photo, including:

The newsfeed of your followers

You should be designing your profile picture for THAT location. It is great to have these fancy profile images that work alongside your cover photo, but if it does not work in the newsfeed then you need to scrap the idea and start again. You need to ask yourself, is my brand recognized in the newsfeed?

Hot tip

Make sure your profile picture fits in the space provided.

Don't forget

If your logo is not visible in the newsfeed, then change your profile picture.

Posts on your page's timeline

Every time you post on your timeline, or reply to a comment, it is your avatar/profile picture that is displayed.

Comments and posts you make on other pages while using your page

The techniques in commenting and liking other pages are discussed later in the chapter, but you can see how important a good avatar is if you are keen on letting other businesses know about your brand. If the logo does not fit correctly, or if you are unable to read it on the timeline then not only are you missing a valuable brand awareness opportunity, but you are also showing less care for your Facebook followers.

We will be there!|

Tips for creating a great looking profile picture that your audience will recognize immediately:

- Use your logo if you have one
- Minimize or eliminate all text if possible
- If you are a business or brand, don't use a headshot, unless you are your brand
- Do not change it very often, as consistency is the name of the game here (but change your cover photo)
- Use an image that is recognizable, and consistent with your other social networking platforms
- Never, ever use stock photos
- Make sure it's square (which I appreciate is easier said than done for some businesses)

Facebook applications

To make your page stand out from the crowd use some of the Facebook applications (apps).

Here is how Facebook describes an application:

"Apps are designed to enhance your experience on Facebook with engaging games and useful features. You can use apps to listen to music with friends, share what you're reading, play games and more. Explore and add apps from the App Center to find games and social apps that fit your interests".

What are some of the most popular apps that you can add to your Facebook page?

eBay or Amazon – with this handy little app that has been added to your Facebook page, consumers can purchase directly from your shop without leaving Facebook. (There are many e-commerce type of apps.)

If your business often gets asked a lot of the same questions, then why not add a Frequently Asked Questions tab?

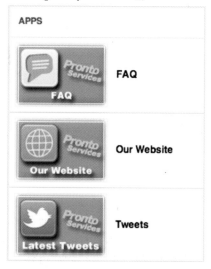

Beware

You can only add applications to your Facebook page if your account is connected to a personal profile. If it is not connected to a personal profile then you are very limited in the functionality of your page.

...cont'd

If you work in the recruitment world or perhaps you are part of a larger organization that is constantly recruiting, then consider adding a jobs board to your Facebook page. Jobs boards can be interactive, and potential job seekers can view and apply for jobs, right from your Facebook page.

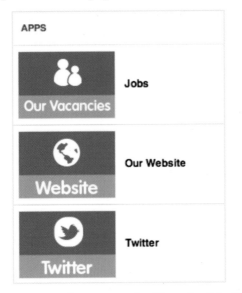

One of the most popular apps is the "live chat" facility. This app would be fabulous for any industry that offers a free helpline such as IT or legal services.

If you have a popular YouTube channel, then why not market those creative videos using the YouTube app on your Facebook page? Some of the apps will automatically post new videos on your timeline.

How do I add an application to my Facebook page?
There are a number of ways in which to add applications to your Facebook page. You can visit the app center for pages at **https:// www.facebook.com/appcenter/category/pageapps**

Not all applications on Facebook are up-to-date with the latest Facebook developments. Therefore, not all Facebook applications will work on your Facebook page.

...cont'd

The app center is a little bit like the iTunes store or Google Play store. Unlike iTunes or Google Play it is much easier to have an application approved on Facebook. Facebook is not as strict with the developers as iTunes or Google Play; therefore, you will often find that many applications no longer work as they have not been updated by the developer to keep up-to-date with new enhancements that Facebook has made.

The best way to add an application is to acquire it from another page, as you already know that the app works absolutely fine.

Not all apps work this way, but a good percentage do. Here is how you acquire an app from another page:

1 Find the application that you wish to add to your page

2 Click on the app, then scroll down to the very bottom. You will find a link that may say **Get this app** or **Add this app to your page**, or **Powered by...**

3 Simply click on the link and follow the instructions online. Each application is different and will have different instructions

There are many Facebook app developers but not all are able to stay up-to-date with Facebook. However, the following developers seem to have the most popular applications and tend to keep up with frequently changing Facebook developments:

- **Woobox** – helps you easily create powerful contests, sweepstakes, coupons, and more to grow your fans and amplify your marketing. Visit their site at **http://woobox.com/**
- **Pagemodo** – Create contests, sweepstakes, coupons, contact forms, product display tabs and so much more. Visit their site at **http://www.pagemodo.com/**

Have fun with these applications. You will likely add some apps and then delete them after a few months, in the same way that you do with your smartphone. However, introducing new and exciting functions on a regular basis on your page is not a bad thing, so enjoy and have some fun with them.

> **Have you added any applications to your Facebook page? Then you are awarded one point!**

Have fun and experiment with applications on your page.

Branded custom applications

How do you brand applications?

 Click on **Settings**

Page	Activity **1**	Insights	Settings

 Click on **Apps**

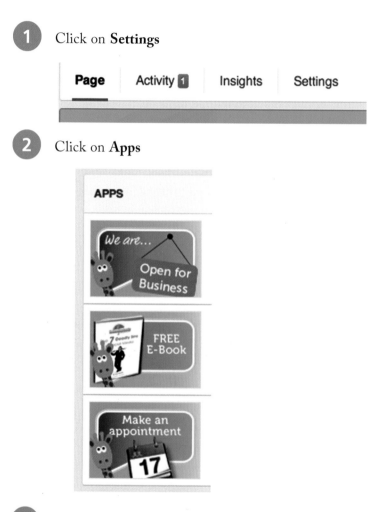

 Click **Edit settings** on the relevant application that you wish to change

In the edit area, you have the option to change the name of the application, as well as changing the design of the icon.

4   Click on **Change** and then select the image (image size – 111 pixels wide x 74 pixels deep) that you would like to upload to replace the default image supplied by the application developer

As an administrator of your page, you can also swap the apps around. We suggest that you change them around on a fairly regular basis so that your other applications have a chance of being viewed.

...cont'd

To reorganize your applications:

 Click **More**

 Click **Manage Tabs**

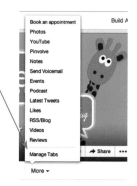

 Drag the applications into your preferred order of priority

There are a number of applications that have been created by Facebook which you can add to your page. However, these cannot be branded. These apps are:

- Notes
- Events
- Photos
- Videos
- Reviews

Let's explore these applications in a bit more detail.

Notes

The Notes application is great! It is a very underutilized application, as most businesses are not aware of it.

Facebook Notes is a simple word-processor, often called a blogging platform for Facebook users. While status updates that you post to your timeline have a limited character length (which is often changing), Notes lets you write full-length posts with formatting, tagging and pictures.

Use Notes to publish content that is too long to post to your timeline or that requires formatting.

It is perfect for those who perhaps run a cottage industry business and do not have a website, as you can write articles and full blogs using the Notes facility and publish this content on your other social networking sites.

The main reason for using the Notes facility is that each note that is produced is allocated a unique URL. This means that you can take that URL and post it on your Twitter, Google Plus, LinkedIn accounts, etc. or include a link in an email or on a website.

When you post a Note, it will be shown on your timeline.

Events

The Events tab is also another very underutilized Facebook feature. If you run any conferences, networking events, opening nights, book signings, webinars, Google hangouts, online courses, etc. then this feature is for you.

Hot tip

If you have a slightly longer post, then use the Notes facility.

...cont'd

As with many features in Facebook, there is more than one way to access the information.

 Click on the application that you have installed, then click **Create event**

 OR, visit **www.facebook.com/events** and you get to the same area

You want your event to stand out when you do publish it, so unclick **Publish New Events to Timeline** at the point of creation.

Remove the tick and do NOT publish the event on the timeline at the point of creation

 Go ahead and create your event by completing the form

 Once you have completed your form, click **Create**

Hot tip

Publish events on your timeline after you have completed and checked the details.

5 Click the **Events** tab on the main page

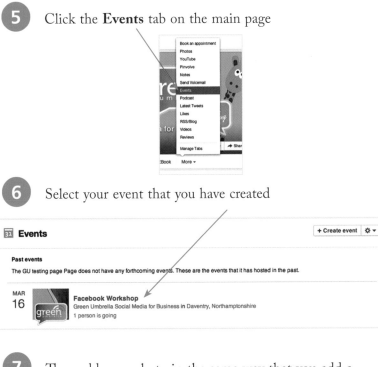

6 Select your event that you have created

Use a system such as Eventbrite (www. eventbrite.com) or Meetup (http://www. meetup.com/) as another way to publicize your event, and an additional way to take payment for events. Publish the links in your Facebook event page.

7 Then add your photo in the same way that you add a Facebook cover photo (covered on pages 86-88). The image size for Facebook's event banners changes quite frequently so check the current size (visit **https://www. facebook.com/CoverPhotoSize**)

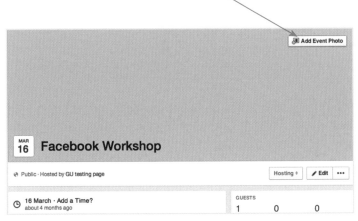

ALWAYS add an image to your events as this has an impact on the marketing of your event.

...cont'd

8 Once you have added your photo, double check that all the information is correct and then invite your Facebook page followers to join your event

The new event comes with its own URL/website address, so you can copy and paste this address as a status update on your personal profile and on your business page. You can also Tweet it, place it on Google Plus, post it in LinkedIn or email the link to your email list etc.

Unique event URL

Photos & Videos

There are numerous ways to add and organize photos and videos to your Facebook page.

Option 1 – is to add a photo/video from the status update area.

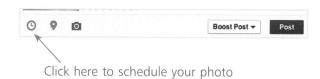

Once the photo has been uploaded, write your status update and either click **Post**, or use the little clock feature to schedule your post for later in the day.

Click here to schedule your photo

Hot tip

The little clock will only appear if you have "switched" and you are posting as your business page. It will not appear if you are posting as your personal profile.

Option 2 – post from the photos area.

It is best to post from this area if you are posting a group of photos and you wish to have them all in one album. For example, you may have taken a lot of photos at your Christmas party, or perhaps at a training day or annual conference. Posting these as individual photos on your timeline will simply flood your readers' newsfeed, and it is not recommended.

How do you create an album for your photos on Facebook?

1 Click on **More**

2 Click on **Photos**

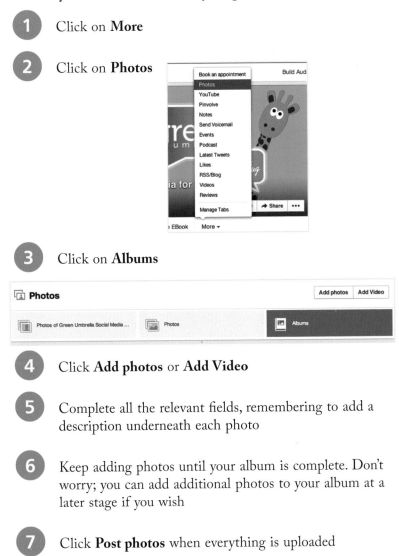

3 Click on **Albums**

4 Click **Add photos** or **Add Video**

5 Complete all the relevant fields, remembering to add a description underneath each photo

6 Keep adding photos until your album is complete. Don't worry; you can add additional photos to your album at a later stage if you wish

7 Click **Post photos** when everything is uploaded

...cont'd

Chocolate Album (5 photos)
This is a test album for my book. — at Green Umbrella Social Media for Business

Like · Comment · Share · Assign To

If you are posting and utilizing the photo albums, it is displayed like this on your timeline, which looks so much better than posting 20 photos in a row.

Hot tip

You can upload photos to your Facebook page in bulk.

Option 3 – using your smartphone.

You can upload photos to the Facebook business page using the Facebook applications. However, there is an application called iLoader, which is available for iOS and Android. Visit the website **http://www.tektrify.com/iloader/**

What do I like about iLoader?

If I am uploading images to my or a clients' business page, it is usually in bulk as I will be at an event or conference of some kind.

Here are some of the cool features of this application:

● Upload videos or photos to your profile or page in bulk.
● Add captions to your image and tag people or businesses.
● Enhance the images using special effects.
● Add a frame or border to your image to make them look professional.

- Add stickers to your image.
- Reduce redeye, remove blemishes.
- If you have no Internet, it is not a problem. iLoader can plan all your images offline and then it will upload when you do have a Wi-Fi connection.
- You can add memes. A meme is when you add words to a picture, a bit like this:

Then with a click of a button the images are posted!

Is your Facebook page adequately branded? If you have changed your cover photo on a regular basis, your avatar works well in the newsfeed and you have branded your custom apps, then you deserve a full point! If you have only completed a few of these, then give yourself half a point.

How to produce excellent content

Before we discuss what content works best on a Facebook page, let's have a look at how the Facebook algorithm (known as EdgeRank) works.

edgerank

Web definitions

EdgeRank is the name commonly given to the algorithm that Facebook uses to determine what articles should be displayed in a user's News Feed. ...
http://en.wikipedia.org/wiki/EdgeRank

Don't forget

Not everyone who "likes" your page will see all of your posts.

Did you know that you do not see all your friends' posts in your newsfeed? It is the people that you interact with the most, or the popular posts from your friends that are published to your newsfeed.

If you have 200 friends, you may only see a small selection of posts in the feed. And it is the same with a business page.

You may have 10,000 likes on your page, but it is the smaller figure next to it that you should be taking note of. This area is called People Talking About This (PTAT). This is the number of people who are seeing your posts on the page, and it takes hard work, lots of engagement, and perhaps lots of money by paying for adverts to keep this at an acceptable level.

People Talking About This is the most important figure

The importance of PTAT is discussed on pages 121-122.

When it comes to content on your page, it is best to adhere to Pareto's Principle, otherwise known as the 80/20 rule.

Wikipedia explanation:

The distribution is claimed to appear in several different aspects relevant to entrepreneurs and business managers. For example:

- 80% of a company's profits come from 20% of its customers
- 80% of a company's complaints come from 20% of its customers
- 80% of a company's profits come from 20% of the time its staff spend
- 80% of a company's sales come from 20% of its products
- 80% of a company's sales are made by 20% of its sales staff[9]

Therefore, many businesses have an easy access to dramatic improvements in profitability by focusing on the most effective areas and eliminating, ignoring, automating, delegating or retraining the rest, as appropriate.

Abide by the 80/20 rule at all times and you can't go wrong.

Implementing this rule into social media and Facebook content marketing:

20% of everything that you post onto Facebook should be "branded content". This means content that will educate your audience about your products, your service, your brand, etc. Below is an example of 20% content.

20%

Events

Features of your services

Links to your blog

Tips on your industry

Promoting special offers

Benefits of your products

Links to "meet the team"

This content will attract a number of likes, comments and shares.

...cont'd

But Facebook is a SOCIAL network, with an emphasis on the word "social".

Remember the EdgeRank calculation. Only people that interact and engage with your posts will see your content (unless you pay for Facebook advertising). Therefore, 80% of your posts should be to encourage conversation from your audience. We jokingly call this type of post "beans on toast".

Let me explain.

A few years ago, I was just about to tuck into my lunch of beans on toast with cheese on top. My designer pointed out that cheese on top of the beans was just wrong and that you really should have cheese on toast, with the beans on the top. A heated discussion broke out in the office, so I took a picture of my lunch and posted it on my Facebook page with the message, "Heated discussion in the office today: Beans on toast – cheese on top or underneath?" The conversation online was lively!

Another successful post was to ask the audience their opinion on which pens we should have branded. We took five random pens, placed them on white card and wrote 1, 2, 3, 4, 5 underneath them. We then asked our audience to vote on which pen we should have branded.

The volume of comments pleasantly surprised us.

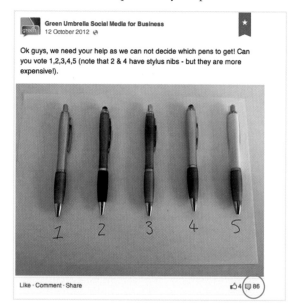

I can hear you thinking to yourself, "What on earth has this type of message got to do with a business page that represents a social media marketing agency?"

Remembering the EdgeRank algorithm, all of those people who are interacting with our business page will also see the 20% posts that make a difference. If you fail to get interaction on the page, then you are limited to the number of people that will see your posts in their newsfeed.

The idea is to find out what makes your audience tick, and to keep that going.

All the people who commented on the page will also see the 20% posts

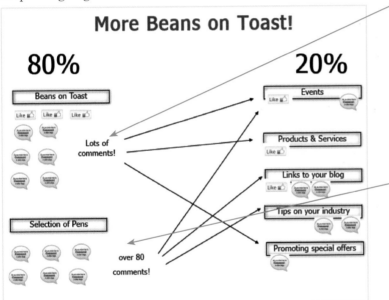

The interaction on the pens post means over 80 people will also see the links to the blog in their newsfeed

Here are some examples of good "beans on toast" posts:

- Open ended questions
- Fill in the blank
- Behind the scenes (is it someone's birthday in the office?)
- Quotes
- Quizzes – guess the object
- Trivia
- Welcoming people to your page
- Family and pets
- Videos and tips

...cont'd

- Funny/humorous
- Pictures from events or trade fairs
- Seasonal posts

It is worth noting that Facebook frowns upon "like-baiting". Like-baiting is when you ask for comments, likes and shares within the post. Facebook knows that you are trying to manipulate the system.

A few examples of a "like-baiting" post would be something like:

By a show of LIKES, how many people would dress up their pets with Holiday reindeers?

[First Sunday in Feb] It's Super Bowl Time! Will it be [team] or [team]? Tell us in the comments!

Click LIKE if the first site you go to in the morning is Facebook... leave a COMMENT if not and tell us the first site you go to.

These types of posts are big no-nos!

There are a variety of tools that can help you with good content ideas. One of the main tools is: Post planner (**https://apps. facebook.com/postplanner/)**. It is a fabulous tool which has four main areas:

- **Status Ideas Engine** – get proven status ideas that get tons of likes and comments and share them instantly on Facebook, or schedule them for later in the week, month or year.

Beware

Like-baiting is frowned upon by Facebook.

post ⦿ planner
Save 2 Hours Daily on Facebook

- **Viral Photos Engine** – is fantastic! Everything from famous quotes to beautiful and engaging photography that you can click a button and post to your profile or page.
- **Trending Content** – post the hottest and freshest content in your niche and add any keyword.

...cont'd

- **Content Engine** – create your own "content firehose", with the hottest content from your favorite Fan Pages, Blogs and Twitter feeds.
- **Discover NEW Content Sources** – discover awesome blogs and experts in your niche.

Another good source for more humorous or personal profile content on Facebook is an application within Facebook called Status Shuffle: **https://apps.facebook.com/status-shuffle/**

Status Shuffle   **Shuffle**   Images   Favorites   Add Your Own   Go Pro | Invite Friends | Help

Status update tactics

The status update is probably the most powerful tool to use on Facebook. Here are some tactics to consider when posting an update:

- Tagging people and other businesses in a post
- Using highlighted posts (not available on the brand new timeline)
- Using pinned posts
- Posting images
- Posting videos
- Scheduling posts
- Deleting the URL after you have imported the website address

Are you adding "beans on toast" to your page? If your page has a variety of content which mixes the 20% content (sales and broadcast messages) with 80% content (behind the scenes, humorous posts, sharing others' content) as well as videos, images and text-based posts, then congratulations, you can give yourself a point.

Adding milestones

Adding life events or milestones to your business page is a great way to promote your company's history to showcase your achievements. You can find a list of your life events in the "About" area of your Facebook page.

How do you add a milestone to your page?

If you do not have many (or any) milestones in your Facebook page then you can backdate your posts. Do not worry; you will not flood your timeline by adding posts in the past. If you post a milestone for 1989, then it will appear in the **About** area, but will also post on your timeline for 1989, instead of the date that you posted it.

To add a milestone for your business, you must be logged in as your page (so remember to "switch" – see page 81). You may not have **Offer** on your page; so just click the last tab on the status update area (it will probably say **Event**). Then click on **Milestone**.

Some ideas of milestones for your business could be:

- When your business was established
- When new locations are opened
- Staff promotions
- Working with a new sector
- When you establish important partnerships
- Brand new website
- When you have gained important accreditations
- When you receive awards or recognitions
- Launch of new products or services
- Celebrating numbers of likes
- Welcoming new staff

Ensure that you complete all relevant areas of the milestone page for maximum impact, including images and a story to support the event.

Do you have milestones added to your Facebook page? If you have more than four milestones then give yourself a point.

Like other businesses

Having a Facebook page that is not engaged with other businesses is a bit like going to a wedding with an empty dance floor. You need to get up and start the party if you want it to be vibrant, and your Facebook page is no different.

Take a look and see if your business "likes" other businesses.

From the image below, you can see that this page called Pets Located (*https://www.facebook.com/PetsLocated*) has a target market of people who are animal lovers. Therefore, they need to interact and engage with this audience. Rather than waiting for people to find their page, they have "liked" lots of other pages that have some synergy with their own page. When you click on the redirect/greater than tab, there are a number of businesses that they like to engage with.

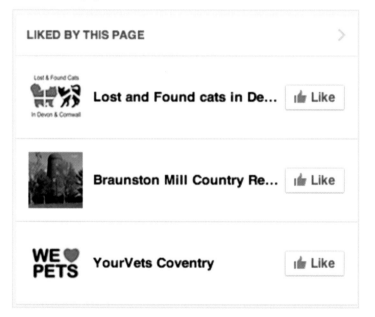

Liking other pages is not enough though. You need to start interacting and engaging with the other pages and their audience.

How do you like other pages and start engaging with them?

 You need to find the pages

There are some glitches in Facebook and sometimes if you

are searching for a page when you are logged in as the business, then it may not appear in the search results. You can switch back to your personal profile and then conduct a search.

Alternatively, a good solution to find pages is to simply enter a search into Google, remembering to add the keyword "Facebook".

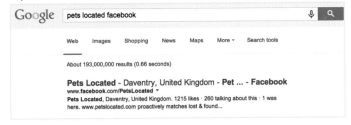

2 Copy the URL of the page that you intend to like

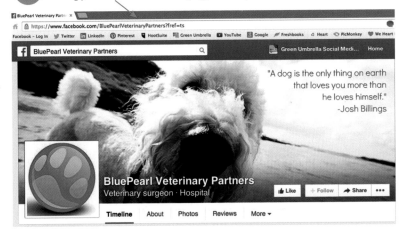

...cont'd

 Switch to your business page

Don't forget

You are now viewing the page that you would like to engage with as your business, rather than as your personal profile. Is your page name displayed at the top right hand corner? If it is displaying your personal name, then go back to Step 3.

 Paste the URL into the address bar

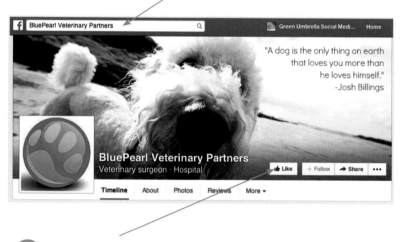

5 Click **Like** on the page

6 Start engaging with the pages that you have liked

The next stage is to comment, like and share posts from your Home tab.

Simply click **Home** and scan the newsfeed of the pages that you have liked.

If there are particular posts with lots of comments (like the one on the next page from Raspberry Pi's Facebook page) then these should ideally be the posts that you should engage with. Remember, everyone within that thread will receive a notification, giving your business further brand awareness with your target audience.

Limit your number of shares, comments and likes to a maximum of five a day, and try not to do this activity all in one go otherwise you will flood your newsfeed.

Comment, like or share as your business

If your business has "liked" more than six other pages, then give yourself a point in the score chart at the end of this chapter.

Is your page name indexable?

Does your page appear in search results on Facebook and also on Google?

Keywords

Beware

As mentioned earlier, once you have reached 200 likes, then you are unable to change your page name without sending documents to support the change to Facebook support. This process can sometimes be quick, but other times it may take a few weeks.

First, let's talk about being found on the Facebook search.

● Don't worry if your new page is not found immediately on Facebook, it usually takes approximately 2-3 days before Facebook indexes new pages. The more likes, engagement and interaction your page has, then the higher it will appear in search engines.

● Ensure that your page name includes a keyword about your business or location. Prevention is better than cure, so make sure your page name includes searchable keywords for your business in the page name. e.g. Our page name now reads "Green Umbrella Social Media for Business".

To edit your Facebook page name

1   Click **Settings**

2   Click **Page Info**

3   Click the small pencil next to **Edit** alongside the business name

Let's see what parts of your Facebook page are indexed by Google.

 Visit: **https://www.facebook.com/username**

In the example below, the username of Mari Smith (a well known Facebook guru) has been typed in. You can see from the results that at the time of writing this book, Mari Smith's Facebook page has been indexed 12,900 times by Google.

Now this is the clever bit. If you look at the top entries on the search results you will see what pages are indexed most by Google.

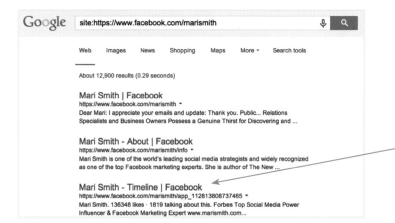

Mari Smith has an extremely active application on her Facebook page which links to something that she was previously selling (it is no longer available, but this information tells how successful it was).

The key to social media success is to constantly evolve and give your audience what they want. Analyzing some of the key areas of your Facebook page will give you the knowledge of where you are going wrong or what you are doing right, so that you can change your strategy to make it better.

> **Is your page indexable? Do you have keywords within the name of your page? If yes, then feel free to add a little tick in the box for this section in the chart at the end of this chapter.**

Pass the LikeAlyzer test

LikeAlyzer helps you to measure and analyze the potential and success rate of your Facebook page, and it is completely free of charge. We use this as a tool to see what our clients' competitors are scoring to keep ahead of the game.

Visit **http://likealyzer.com/** by Meltwater to find your results.

Let's see what the guru herself, Mari Smith's LikeAlyzer score is.

As you can see, her Facebook page scores quite high, with a ranking of 74. Your LikeAlyzer score can change from day-to-day.

Review of Mari Smith

They have given suggestions as to how she can get a higher score on her Facebook page, such as adding milestones to the page, have better timing of the posts, mixing up the variety of types of posts and responding quicker to her audience. Even the gurus have room for improvement.

So what was your score on your LikeAlyzer test? If you scored higher than 50, then give yourself a point in the checklist at the end of the chapter.

What is your PTAT Score?

If you have read the section on EdgeRank (see pages 106-111), then you will appreciate the importance of engagement on your page. If no-one is engaging with your business, then your posts will not be shown in the newsfeed of your fans. In short, if you do not post interesting and engaging content, then no-one will see any of your posts.

How do you know what your People Talking About This (PTAT) score is?

1   Click the > on the People tab

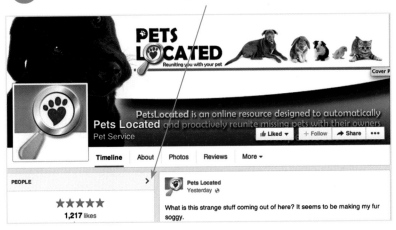

2   View your PTAT figure

...cont'd

According to Facebook, the following different types of actions are included in the algorithm to measure in your PTAT score:

- People actually "liking" your page.
- Liking, commenting on, or sharing your post. A like does not have as much weight in the algorithm as a comment, and a comment does not have as much weight in the algorithm as a share (the more shares the better).
- Responding to your event.
- Mentioning your page (when a business "tags" you in a post).
- When people "Check In".
- New recommendations or reviews.
- Original posts from your audience on your page.

You will notice that this list does include people who have liked your page. If you are running a Facebook advert campaign then you will need to be aware of this. Once your advert has commenced you will suddenly see a spike in your PTAT statistics, even if your fans are not interacting with your page. Thus, it is important to look at your PTAT net of the paid fans you are acquiring.

A good PTAT score is anything more than 10%. They say that Facebook cap the PTAT to 16%, but I have not seen any proof of this. It is also extremely difficult to continuously keep your PTAT score above 16% without putting your hand in your pocket and paying for adverts. (To find your percentage, using the page example shown on page 121, take the PTAT figure (208), then divide by the number of likes (1570), then multiply by 100).

To increase your PTAT score, then refer to pages 106-111 on EdgeRank and master your content strategy.

Don't forget

You can run Facebook Advertisement campaigns for which you have to pay. This book covers free online marketing.

> **What is your PTAT percentage? If you have scored above 10% then give yourself a tick in the check box at the end of this chapter.**

Conclusion

In conclusion, having a Facebook page can be very rewarding for a business. Let's look at the four steps to Facebook success:

1 **Build your platform**

If you have branded your account, added applications, grabbed your URL, changed your page name and completed the About area, then you should be confident in saying that you have reached stage one for Facebook success for a small business owner.

2 **Grow your network**

As previously mentioned, if you have no likes, or no interaction on your page then you are really just talking to yourself which is the first sign of madness! Have you reached a reasonable number of likes for your niche market, and are those people interacting on your page? If so, then you have reached stage two of Facebook success for the small business owner.

3 **Implement a Strategy**

Have you defined your target market? Do you like other pages in your industry and your key target audience? Do you know the best time to post? Have you defined your 80/20 content strategy? Are you using hashtags in your posts and mixing up the variety of posts, i.e. images, videos, text, etc? If you have a defined strategy to achieve your Facebook goals and objectives, then well done! You have achieved stage three Facebook success for a small business owner.

4 **Measure the Results**

There are many ways in which to measure the results for Facebook, but the easiest way is to use the Facebook Insights which are found in the Admin Panel. Products such as Hootsuite, SproutSocial and other software can also produce statistics for you. If you measure your results, tweaking your strategy and then measuring again the following month, then give yourself a pat on the back as you have reached stage four of Facebook success for a small business owner.

Checklist

It's time to be totally honest now and have a look at your score for your Facebook page.

1 Is your "About" area completed in full?

2 Have you grabbed your unique URL?

3 Branding – if you have branded your cover photo, avatar and custom application icons, then give yourself a point.

4 Are you utilizing applications to enhance your Facebook page?

5 If your page has some great content with a variety of images, videos, text posts as well as a mix of 20% content and 80% type of content then please award yourself a point for content.

6 Do you have four or more milestones on your page?

7 Does your page "like" more than six other businesses?

8 Is your page name indexable?

9 Do you have a higher score than 50 on the LikeAlyzer test?

10 What is your percentage of PTAT? (People Talking About This). If you have a greater score than 10% PTAT then you are awarded a point.

One could write a whole book on Facebook, but the above check points are really a good starting point for all small business owners. How did you score out of 10?

5 Twitter

Introduction

If you are new to Twitter, then you may be wondering what all the fuss is about. Can it really help small business owners to achieve more sales, gain credibility, and create brand awareness or is it just a waste of time?

I was an early adopter of Twitter and it was only because a few marketing gurus were constantly talking about it that I decided to give it a try and see if it would work for my small local recruitment business.

Here are seven reasons why you should be using Twitter if you are a small business owner:

Don't forget

Twitter is a fast way to publish your message to the world.

1 More people are using Twitter

The local corner shop owner, the landscape gardener, accountant, solicitor, the local golf club, the job seeker, the property hunter, and all sorts of people. Along with hundreds of large corporate companies, who will be advertising their tender opportunities and so much more.

Having your business on Twitter is popular and you will be amazed how many opportunities you could be missing by not being a part of this world. If you are a local business, and perhaps you are already attending business-networking breakfasts such as BNI (Business Networking International), FSB (Federation of Small Businesses) or business lunches, then Twitter is certainly a platform not to ignore.

2 The Cool Factor

Using Twitter is evidence that your small business is participating in this whole social media thing and is obviously a "with-it" company that people might be interested in doing business with. It's just not enough to have a website nowadays.

3 A fast way to get your message published

Assuming your potential and existing customers are on Twitter, you can instantly let them know your news, whether it's an announcement of a new product, a special deal, or an upcoming event they may be interested in.

4 **Keep updated with industry news**
Twitter lets you hear what other people are saying. Using Twitter Search or their advanced search you can find out what people are saying about a particular topic, enabling you to keep your ear to the ground about your company and, of course, your competition.

5 **Enhance your brand awareness**
By participating in Twitter (that is, using it to communicate with others, rather than just spamming product announcements and constantly broadcasting) you can present and develop the kind of image that attracts your potential clients. (Remember; communication is a two-way dialogue, not a monologue). Branding of your Twitter account is discussed as part of the 10-point checklist.

6 **Twitter opens opportunities to speak to high profile people/companies**
Being on Twitter will give you opportunities to meet and talk to an unlimited number of people, some of whom you would never get the chance to talk to otherwise. And some of those people might be the very business contacts you've been seeking; people you want to start projects with, source products from or even recruit for your business.

7 **The perfect tool for customer retention**
Posting information about your products and/or services is the obvious use. But Twitter also gives you another channel for listening to and finding out about your customers – what they like or dislike about you or your company, how they feel about your brand, what suggestions they have for improvement, what their favorite products are and why... all kinds of nuggets that you can use to make your business more successful.

Twitter can provide your small business with another channel to inform and engage your current and potential customers – and every opportunity to do that is worth exploring.

Creating your Twitter profile

Before you launch yourself into Twitter, you must first abide by Step 1 to social media success and build your platform. Twitter is the easiest of platforms to create a profile for as the information is limited.

To create your Twitter profile:

1 Visit **www.twitter.com** and complete the online prompts

2 When registering your account you do not need to "follow" all the people as prompted; simply click on the X on each suggested person

3 During the online registration process, always check your location, as the default can be a random location. This is found in the Edit Profile area

4 Do not protect your Tweets as this limits your visibility

5 You will be sent an email to verify the account – make sure you click on the link to confirm your Twitter account

You can change your username at any time.

The 10 key elements of how to build your Twitter account and the tools and techniques that can help enhance your Twitter presence are illustrated in the following pages. As you go along, tick the boxes at the end of the chapter and see what your score is.

Branding your Twitter account

You don't have to be a big brand like Pepsi or Virgin Media to brand your Twitter account, so take a look at the two main areas in which you can brand your Twitter account.

The avatar (profile picture)

The principals for branding your avatar are simple. Depending on the type of business you're in either use a photo of yourself or a company logo. If you decide to add a company logo then ensure that it fits correctly and it is not too busy. This is the part of your brand that will communicate with other Twitter users throughout the day.

Twitter avatar

Hot tip

Square logos or head and shoulder photos work much better than rectangular logos.

Your avatar needs to work in the newsfeed as well

Tweets	Tweets and replies

Julia Doherty @JuliaDoherty · 2h
Nordic walking this morning Check it out!
facebook.com/photo.php?fbid...

Profile Picture: 73 x 73 pixels. The maximum file size that you can upload is 500 x 500 pixels. This is what users will see when they actually click on your profile picture. When your profile picture appears in someone's timeline, it will be resized to 24 x 24 pixels. Bear these sizes in mind when creating a Twitter avatar.

Does your avatar work? If you have a logo that is very long, it is very difficult to incorporate it into a profile picture for it to be effective. Square logos certainly work much better.

...cont'd

To change your Twitter profile picture

 Click on **Edit profile**

 Click **Change your profile photo**

 Upload your new profile picture

The Twitter header

The Twitter header is an exceptionally important feature, as this is one of the main branding elements that appear on smartphone applications. The header was introduced in September 2012, and has been updated in size in April 2014. Therefore, if you branded your account before these dates, then your Twitter header will appear as a black, blank screen, or may look distorted.

Header

Header Image: Twitter recommends dimensions of 1500 pixels in width x 500 pixels in height.

To change your Twitter header

Click on **Edit profile**

Click **Change your header photo**

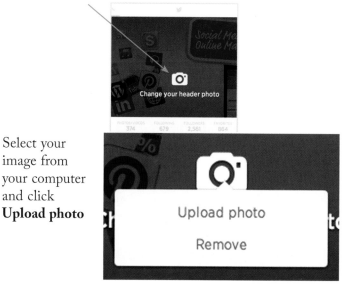

Select your image from your computer and click **Upload photo**

Upload photo

Remove

The size of the Twitter header changed in April 2014. Therefore, to see if your header is distorted, just click the small avatar in the top right corner, then click View profile.

Don't forget

131

What does your Twitter account say about you? Does your avatar work well; is your header branded and consistent with all other platforms online? If "yes", then congratulations! You are awarded a point in the checklist at the end of this chapter.

A healthy follower/following ratio

There is only one reason why some Twitter users follow hundreds of people, and that is to simply increase the number of people that follow them back. It is very easy to get large numbers of Twitter followers if you simply use this tactic, but quality far outweighs quantity every time.

Here are three reasons why following everyone back is a pointless task:

Twitter spam

The more people you follow, the more you are open to Twitter spam.

I joined Twitter in 2009, and in those early days I was keen to get 100s of followers as quickly as possible. All the blog articles I read were encouraging me to follow people, up to an additional 100 people every day, so that is what I did. Yes, I soon got into the hundreds quite quickly, but with this came additional work for me.

With Twitter, if you follow someone, you are giving that person the green light to send you a DM (Direct Message). Every day I was receiving spam messages: "Follow our Facebook page", "Have you checked out our website?", "Buy the latest gadget" etc. It got to a point where I simply had to unfollow lots of people, and risk the chance that my own following might decrease – which it did.

The question I needed to ask myself was, if people are only following me because I am following them, does that mean that they are not really interested in the content that I am providing? Is it just a numbers game? From mid 2009, I made the decision to ONLY follow people that I am genuinely interested in talking to. Yes, I may not have thousands and thousands of followers, but I know that the people who are following me are genuinely interested in the content that I am providing, and this far outweighs the value of having thousands of followers who are not listening to anything I am Tweeting.

Missing important Tweets

Picture the scene: You are following 1700 people. Your newsfeed is manic and full of noise. You log in to Twitter twice a day. How on earth do you keep in touch with the people that really count – your target market? You may be using lists (hopefully you are – see pages 136-140) to manage the people that you are following, but if you are following people that you have no intention of communicating with then what's the point of following them?

Twitter will tell you off

If you use the tactic of "follow loads of people so that they follow me back", then you will not be seen favorably in Twitter's eyes. If your ratio of followers is substantially lower than your following then Twitter will suspend your account.

Beware

If your ratio of followers is substantially lower than your following then Twitter will suspend your account.

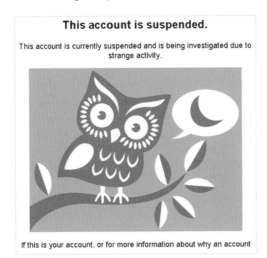

This account is suspended.

This account is currently suspended and is being investigated due to strange activity.

If this is your account, or for more information about why an account

If you are not yet convinced that this is NOT a good method of increasing your Twitter followers, then here is an extract from Twitter's rules:

Twitter's technical follow limits

Every account can follow 2,000 users total. Once you've followed 2,000 users, there are limits to the number of additional users you can follow. This number is different for each account and is based on your ratio of followers to following; this ratio is not published. Follow limits cannot be lifted by Twitter and everyone is subject to limits, even high profile and verified celebrity accounts.

Every Twitter account is technically unable to follow more than 1,000 users per day, in addition to the account-based limits above. Please note that this is just a technical limit to prevent egregious abuse from spam accounts.

Accounts are also prohibited from aggressively following other users. Our Following rules and best practices page (https://support. Twitter.com/entries/68916) has more information on Twitter's following rules.

...cont'd

Make sure that you have a healthy following/follower ratio.

Take advice from the celebrities. If you look at any of their accounts you will notice that the number of followers will far supersede the number of people that the individuals are following.

Here are a couple of examples of unhealthy following/follower ratio. You can see that the first account initially appears quite vibrant with nearly 42,000 followers. However, looking at the volume of people being followed (45,000), it makes you wonder how many of those 45K people are actually listening to anything that is being Tweeted here, or is it just a numbers game?

TWEETS	PHOTOS/VIDEOS	FOLLOWING	FOLLOWERS	FAVORITES	
14.7K	85	45.9K	41.7K	140	More ⌄

Unhealthy following/follower ratio

Looking at the second example, they also have an unhealthy following/follower ratio. Given that they have only Tweeted 1,553 times since their account was launched then following thousands of people to get that huge following has probably been a key strategy for this account.

TWEETS	PHOTOS/VIDEOS	FOLLOWING	FOLLOWERS	FAVORITES	
1,553	17	44.6K	40.5K	5	More ⌄

Unhealthy following/follower ratio

Let's have a look at some healthy accounts.

Healthy

		TWEETS	PHOTOS/VIDEOS	FOLLOWING	FOLLOWERS	FAVORITES	
		14.8K	233	2,981	182K	100	More ⌄

Environment Agency ✔
@EnvAgency

Tweets   Tweets and replies

Retweeted by Environment Agency

You will see that this is an excellent Twitter account with a very healthy follower/following ratio. They have 182,000 followers and they are only following 2,981 people, which suggests that they have over 179,000 followers who are following them because they are interested in the content that they are Tweeting out to the world. They are not following them because @envAgency is following them back.

Celebs always have the best ratio, and you can see by Alan Sugar's Twitter account that he has over 3 million followers, but he is only following a mere 483 people.

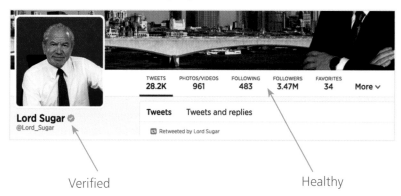

Verified

Healthy

Don't forget

If you follow hundreds, or thousands of people, then your newsfeed will be very noisy!

It is worth noting that if an account has a blue tick next to the name, then this represents a genuine and authentic account, and it is awarded by Twitter itself – this is not something that you can request to be added. To find out more about verified accounts then visit **http://www.Twitter.com/help/verified**

Using Twitter lists

Twitter lists are underutilized. It is difficult to imagine how a user can follow more than 100 people without using Twitter lists. How would you keep on top of who is saying what in one long newsfeed, without being on Twitter 24/7?

Twitter lists are a great way to organize who you are following (and even who you are NOT following) into groups defined by you.

Here are examples of some of the Twitter lists:

Competitors (private list) – Set up a list of your competitors. You do not have to follow these accounts, just add them to your list. (Unless you have a good relationship with them and you would like to communicate with them.)

Clients (private list) – It is important to make sure that you do not miss any key notices or Tweets from your existing clients.

Target Market (public list) – For example, if you are a supplier to the wine industry, then you may want to have a list for all those potential clients who would be interested in your products. Following vineyards, wine merchants, and having these in one list will keep you focused on your target market.

Press (public list) – Following local press, or perhaps national news, trade magazines, journalists, bloggers in an industry, etc. is always a good source of content ideas for your Twitter account and is worthy of a list.

Famous (public list) – You may want to follow particular sporting personalities, or business gurus etc. I follow a number of thought leaders in my industry, and I have added these to my "Famous" list. I do not check this list every day, but I know it is there, and I check on it a few times a week just to make sure that I do not miss anything important.

How do you create a Twitter list?

As with most platforms, there is always more than one way to achieve the same result and creating a Twitter list is no exception, but here is an easy way to create those all important Twitter lists:

Hot tip

Creating Twitter lists is the easiest way to manage your account on a daily basis.

Hot tip

You do not need to actually "follow" people to put them on a list. Consider this when creating a list for your competitors.

1 Log in to your Twitter account. Click on the avatar on the far right hand side and then click **Lists**

2 Create your list – click on the **Create new list** button

3 Name your list so that it is easily recognized. Complete the description (although this is not always necessary), and then select if this should be a private list (visible to yourself only), or a public list (visible in the public domain for all Twitter users to view and follow). Click **Save list**

Do not add a public list of your clients.

Create a new list	✕
List name	
Description	
	Under 100 characters, optional
Privacy	⦿ Public · Anyone can follow this list
	○ Private · Only you can access this list
	Save list

How do I add people to my list?
Put ALL of the people that you are following into a list.

Visit **https://Twitter.com/following**, which will give you a list of all the people that you are currently following.

...cont'd

1   Click the little cog or gear in the account box

2   Click **Add or remove from lists**

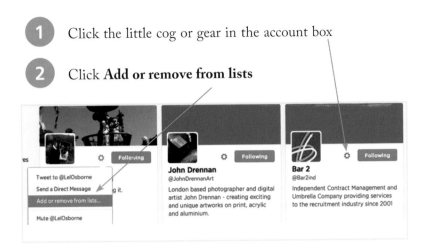

Select which list you would like to allocate this particular account to and then click the **X** in the top right. On occasions, you will find yourself clicking **Create list** in error as it is a natural place for a save button to be, but don't worry, we have all done it!

Develop a habit of adding to your list

Each time you follow a new person then add them to a list. Follow = add to list. If they are not worthy of being added to a list, then you may need to question yourself as to why you are following them in the first place.

What happens if you are put on a public list?

It is nice to know when you have been added to a list. However, you can only be notified if you have been added to a public list.

There are numerous ways to find out if you have been added to a list:

1   Click **More**

2   Click **Lists**. You can see two tabs for **Subscribed to** and **Member of**

Check regularly if you have been put on any new Twitter lists.

3 This is where you can view all the lists that you have created, or other people's lists that you have subscribed to

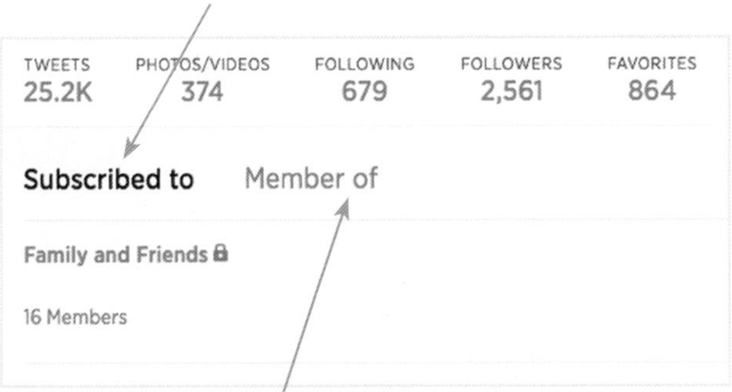

TWEETS	PHOTOS/VIDEOS	FOLLOWING	FOLLOWERS	FAVORITES
25.2K	374	679	2,561	864

Subscribed to   Member of

Family and Friends 🔒

16 Members

4 Clicking on **Member of** will display all the lists that other people have allocated your account to. This is usually quite an interesting exercise to do

Have you been added to any Twitter lists?
If you are using the social media management tool called Hootsuite, (**hootsuite.com**) then this has a built-in service in the smartphone application to notify you if you have been added to any public list, which is exceptionally handy.

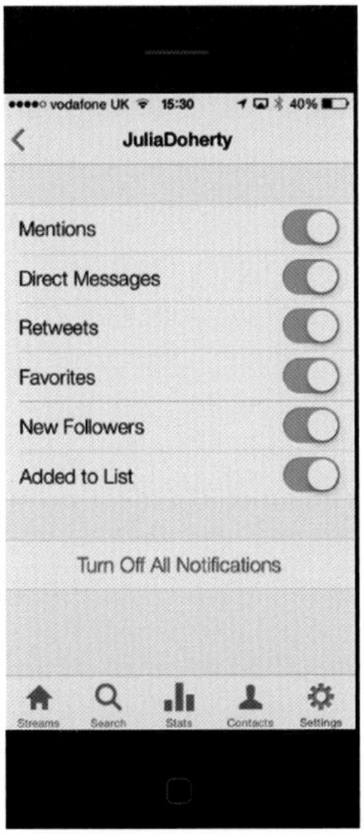

...cont'd

If you are using the Twitter application on your smartphone, then you will see in the notification area when someone has added you to a public list. However, at the time of writing this book you are not currently able to receive these as push notifications.

Deploy the "notice me" strategy

One of the main strategies that we deploy at Green Umbrella is called the "notice me" strategy, which involves the use of Twitter lists.

Set up a "notice me" list on Twitter. On this list you should only have a maximum of 10 key accounts. These are your key prospects that you would like to engage with and ultimately you would like them to follow you back. Each day your objective is to engage with the people in the list. Perhaps re-Tweet them one day, mention them in a Tweet on occasions, give them a Follow Friday (see pages 146-148), and generally make yourself present without annoying them.

If you're taking the time to build a good relationship with a Twitter user, and often re-Tweeting their articles to your network, or saying nice things about them, they will consider following you back over a period of time. Once a person in this list follows you back, they get removed from the list and added to a different list. Then you add your next prospect. The key is to be specific, and to make sure that you have no more than 10 people in this list at any one time.

> **If you are following over 100 people, do you have Twitter lists created? If so, then congratulations, you are awarded a point in the chart at the end of this chapter.**

Registering on Twitter directories

In a similar way to the classic phone book, being listed in the main Twitter directories is a surefire way to help you to be found on Twitter.

There is no guarantee that this will help you to be found, but if an account is registered on a highly popular directory, that is constantly updating its content, then Google will also find you more easily. These directories became popular because they are generally easy to use.

Take advantage of all the options to give you exposure in as many relevant categories as possible. It is one of those tick box exercises, which is a time consuming thing to do, but once done then there is no need to revisit it again for a long time.

Here is a list of the top six Twitter Directories:

- Twellow (**www.twellow.com**) – The Yellow Pages of Twitter, and this is a MUST for any business.

- WeFollow (**www.wefollow.com**) – One of the top Twitter directories, and very user friendly.

- Just Tweet It (**www.justtweetit.com**) – Just Tweet It is a user directory for Twitter organized by genre to allow for users to easily find other Twitter users to connect with.

- TweetFind (**http://www.tweetfind.com/**) – Twitter Directory with Social Listings, Lists & Tools – Bringing together Businesses & Consumers on Twitter.

- TwitterCounter (**www.twittercounter.com**) – The number one stats site powered by Twitter.

- Twibs (**www.twibs.com**) – Twitter business portal, featuring nearly 35,000 businesses that are on Twitter, covering thousands of topics.

Are you registered on the Twitter directories? If so, then congratulations, you have another point in the checklist at the end of this chapter.

Hot tip

Registering with the top six Twitter directories will help you be found on Twitter.

Using hashtags

If you're a Twitter novice, hashtags, those short links preceded by the hash sign (# – otherwise known as a number sign), may seem confusing and pointless. But they are integral to the way we communicate on Twitter, and it's important to know how to use them.

On Twitter, the hash sign (or number sign) turns any word or group of words that directly follow it into a searchable link. The easiest way to describe it, is similar to writing a website address, or an email in a document; it will automatically turn blue. You then know if you click on the blue word, it will automatically send you to the site. Putting a hashtag in front of a word on Twitter will have a similar effect. If you type #50ShadesOfGrey then you will see everyone who is Tweeting about this famous book and you can join in with the conversation.

Here is the Wikipedia description of a hashtag:

> *"Definition: The # symbol, called a hashtag, is used to mark keywords or topics in a Tweet. It was created organically by Twitter users as a way to categorize messages."*

Keep in mind that the @ symbol does something completely different.

Using @ before a person's Twitter name will Tweet that person directly, letting them know you have written to them via the @ Connect feature. A hashtag will not. I will often see messages that say #juliadoherty which is picked up by my listening software, when someone really should have used @juliadoherty instead. If you are trying to contact someone direct, then do not use the hashtag.

You may think that there is a whole list of hashtags somewhere, but in reality there is no pre-set list of hashtags. Create a brand new hashtag simply by putting the hash before a series of words, and if it hasn't been used before, then you can do a little dance! You've invented a hashtag!

Warning! If you are running an event, then make sure that you check out the hashtag to see if anyone is using it before you announce it to the world. (Just enter the hashtag into the

Beware

Using a hashtag in front of someone's name on Twitter will not notify the individual of the Tweet.

Twitter Search facility to see if anyone else is Tweeting using this hashtag). I once ran a conference for over 400 recruiters, utilizing a specific hashtag, only to find that on the very same day, the hashtag was also being used by a lady body building event. Needless to say, the large screen at the conference displaying the Twitter hashtag wall was quite entertaining!

Are there any rules to using a hashtag?

I would highly recommend not using more than two or three hashtags in any one Tweet, otherwise your message will start to reflect a list of keywords rather than an engaging message.

Refrain from hashtagging general words that will not be followed such as #marketing #business. A hashtag is better used when you have something specific in mind such as a location (town, city, country), industry jargon or an event.

Here is an example of a bad use of hashtags. As you can see, the message is completely diluted as you are faced with an array of hashtagged words, which have no real meaning.

#Design education by distance learning. We have trained students in 17 countries! #interiors #landscape #fashion #lighting #furnishing #CAD #DigitalLearning

Look at your last two weeks of Tweets. Are you using hashtags? If the answer is "yes", are you using them in the right context? Congratulations, you have now gained another point in the checklist at the end of the chapter.

Hot tip

Never use any more than three hashtags in any Tweet.

143

Use software to shorten your links so that others can easily re-Tweet your message.

144

Using short URLs

There are many reasons to use a short URL, but first let me give you an example to illustrate what a short URL actually means.

In Twitter, you only have 140 characters. If I wanted to Tweet a link to this website, I would write:

> @juliadoherty How to post a link in a Tweet, click here to find out: https://support.Twitter.com/articles/78124-posting-links-in-a-Tweet

This Tweet is 138 characters, and you can see that the link is dominating the message. If I was using a short URL tool, then it would look more like this:

> @juliadoherty How to post a link in a Tweet, click here to find out: http://ow.ly/tHHKb

This Tweet is 89 characters in length, and leaves room for others to re-Tweet my message to their audience. When Twitter users click on the short link, they will be directed to the long link above, achieving the same objective.

There are two main reasons why we recommend using shortened links in your everyday Tweets.

They make links more manageable

Many website addresses that link to blog posts or articles are long and wordy for SEO (search engine optimization) reasons. One of Google's and other search engines' considerations to SEO are keywords in the URL. This creates a problem for the user. The URLs help describe the content, but are lengthy and are not easy to share on emails, web pages, and especially social media platforms like Facebook, LinkedIn and, of course, Twitter.

URL shorteners help solve the problem of making links more manageable to share. And certain services allow users to add keywords to describe the link.

They can track and compile click data

There are over 100 different URL shortening sites. However, here are four sites to get you started. Most of these sites will provide you with generous statistics:

www.tinyurl.com – Tiny URL is customizable, but has no tracking abilities, it has a toolbar button and a 301 redirect feature.

http://goo.gl/ – This is the Google URL shorterner. URLs and click analytics are public and can be accessed by anyone.

www.bit.ly – This tool is probably the most popular as it saves a copy of the page linked to, tracks "conversations" and offers bookmarking features.

www.ow.ly – Part of the social media management suite called Hootsuite, although you do not need to be a user of this software to use the short URL feature, but you do need to have a Twitter account. You are able to track a variety of statistics using Ow.ly, which is why we favor this particular software above all others.

As Twitter, general social media, and mobile Internet become more popular, the need to make sharing web content easier will increase and should not be ignored. Shorter URLs are becoming more and more integral to that cause.

Are you using short URLs in your Tweets? If so, are you measuring those results and learning from the stats? If "yes", then give yourself a tick in the checklist at the end of this chapter.

Follow Friday strategy

Taken from Mashable article **http://mashable.com/2009/03/06/ Twitter-followfriday/**

What if you didn't know who to follow on Twitter? Would you randomly start following people? Would you follow people you see mentioned by those you already follow? Most likely you would ask your friends for recommendations since you can trust that your friends will suggest people who are worth following. Which is exactly how Follow Friday began.

In mid-January 2009, Follow Friday began with a simple Tweet:

I am starting Follow Fridays. Every Friday, suggest a person to follow, and everyone follow him/her. Today its @fancyjeffrey & @w1redone.

9:53 AM Jan 16th from TweetDeck

 micah
Micah Baldwin

The idea is to think of interesting people you already follow and recommend them to others.

Micah suggested the hashtag #followfriday, and a few friends helped spread the word. On the first Follow Friday, there were almost two #followfriday Tweets per second at its peak.

#FollowFriday: The Trend That Kept Trending.

By Saturday morning, there was no trace of Follow Friday. A one-off fad, perhaps?

Then late the next Thursday night, suddenly #followfriday Tweets began to appear in foreign languages! It seemed that Follow Friday was back. Now, every Friday, people suggest other people to follow.

Why #FollowFriday Works

Follow Friday is successful because of three main factors:

- **It's easy.** It takes little effort to send a Tweet, something people do dozens of times a day.
- **It's participatory.** You don't need to be part of the "Twitterati" to participate. You can suggest one person or 100 people. You can get endorsements from one person or 100 people.
- **It's karmic and it feels good.** It's a great feeling to simply say, "I think this person is great. You should follow them."

Follow Friday strategies can be very powerful if created in a positive way.

Golden Rule for Follow Fridays.

Over time, the Follow Friday (now known as the #ff) has become a tactical strategy for businesses, and there are unwritten rules to follow that make the most of this feature.

Try not to clump people together

By adding a #ff to a long list of @usernames does not offer much credibility to the recipient if they are amongst lots of other names. Producing a Tweet like this on a Friday is not a good idea:

· 1h

#mm @GloriaTalbert, @Jodenecoza, @PoetPatriot, @ilovecrows28, @dw2025rmeat, @flipster48 **#followfriday** by twitnerd.com

It does appear like not much thought has gone into this Tweet. Not only are the names all clumped together with no explanation as to why one should follow them, it is also an automated service produced by **twitnerd.com**, which instantly dilutes any credibility there may have been about following these people.

This next #ff or #FollowFriday is the exact opposite of the above Tweet. Quality is so much better than quantity. If I were the recipient of this Tweet then I would be extremely grateful and would simply have to respond.

The Follow Friday is meant for one person only, and the person Tweeting has gone out of their way to find their video on

...cont'd

YouTube. You can see that this Tweet is more effective and has more credibility than the first one on the previous page:

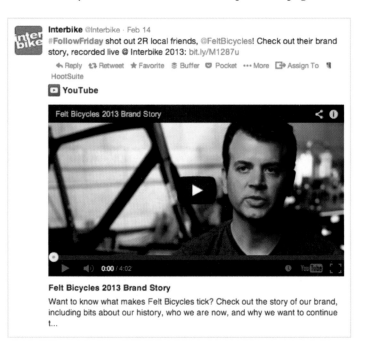

Twitter is all about building relationships and engaging with your audience. A Follow Friday is a very powerful way to achieve this objective as long as it is executed in the right way.

Are you producing weekly #FollowFridays on your Twitter account? If so, do you have a strategy for Follow Fridays? Do you use them to thank new followers? Do you use them to get your name in front of prospects? Perhaps you "Follow Friday" people that you have met within the week? If you do have a strategy for #FollowFridays then please give yourself a tick in the box in the checklist at the end of this chapter.

Social media management tools

Social media is one of the most effective ways for you and your business to get more traffic and generate new leads. Having a presence on all the major platforms like Facebook, Twitter, LinkedIn and Google Plus is a necessity these days for any business. But it is rather time consuming to manage all of these platforms, which is why most business owners who are serious about social media will use a social media management tool.

Why use a social media management tool?

Scheduling your 20% content increases efficiency
Planning your social media, and then scheduling it into a social media management tool makes your life so much easier. If you abide by the 80/20 rule as mentioned in the Facebook chapter, then 20% of your posts can be planned and scheduled across multiple platforms from one place.

Beware, though. You could create all your Tweets on a Sunday for the forthcoming weeks, including thank you messages for future meetings. However, if a meeting was canceled, or rescheduled, you might forget to cancel the Tweet, which could make you look a bit silly. So, only schedule your 20% content. The 80% should be live Tweets.

You will increase your exposure to a larger target market
Engagement and communication are the most important goals to achieve in the Twittersphere. Sure, other metrics apply, but for the most part, if people are complimenting your content, they will share it. So, using a social media management tool allows you to see what your community is saying about your brand, product, or service. It's an amazing listening tool.

A better understanding of social media metrics
This is key for all social media marketers. What good are you as a marketer if you can't deliver a return for your social media marketing efforts? That is a great feature of many social media management tools. They provide you with reporting metrics and other data to help clarify if your efforts had an impact on your social communities.

Eliminate the possibility of spelling and grammar mistakes
All humans make mistakes. It is inevitable. However, there are ways to decrease the margin of error by taking advantage of social

Beware

Never schedule Tweets for appointments as this can get you into trouble.

...cont'd

media marketing tools. By allowing you to post updates and content to multiple channels from one location, you can eliminate any typos or other publishing errors that would normally occur.

Which Social Media Management Tool works best for Twitter?

There are many social media management tools out there to choose from. However, Hootsuite (**www.hootsuite.com**) is a great tool for managing Twitter accounts.

Cost

Hootsuite offers a basic free account allowing you to manage up to three platforms (Facebook, Twitter, LinkedIn, etc). Bearing in mind that if you have a personal Facebook and a business Facebook Page, then two platforms are assigned. Upgrading is not expensive and at the time of going to print, the cost of a professional account is just $9.99 a month. This then gives you unlimited platforms, and you can also manage teams, have enhanced analytics, etc. It is really worth every cent.

User Interface

Hootsuite offers browser-based interface, which has a downloadable app version for Mac users.

Both smartphone and tablet applications are also available.

Hootsuite has a fabulous integration tool called Hootlet, which is a browser extension for Google Chrome and Firefox. This neat little widget allows you to share content instantly from any website to any of your social networking platforms at the click of a button.

Q download the Hootlet extension ---------------->

Another Hootsuite application that we use for Twitter is called HootFeed. This is a fantastic tool if you are running events and wish to create a Twitter wall of your #hashtag Tweets.

The picture below shows a Hootfeed wall for a conference that was held early 2014, which was displayed on huge screens throughout the conference. It is a fantastic way to get people at the conference, and also non-attendees, hyped up about the event.

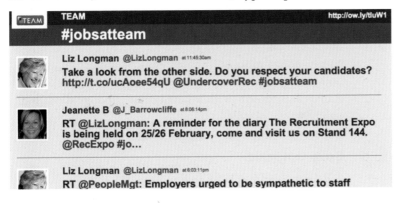

Scheduling updates in advance

There are numerous ways in which you can schedule posts in Hootsuite:

1   **Use the calendar option**, by simply choosing an appropriate date and time. You can amend this at any time by viewing and editing the post in the Publisher section.

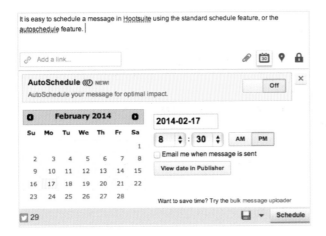

...cont'd

Beware

Never "AutoSchedule" a follow Friday, as they will often be scheduled into a Saturday by the software.

2 Using the AutoSchedule feature

Unfortunately, you cannot specify set times to AutoSchedule. For example, you cannot tell Hootsuite to set your AutoSchedules to go out four times a day at specific times. Hootsuite makes this decision for you by calculating which posts are already pre-scheduled and then populating the AutoSchedules to fill in the gaps. For these types of posts, there is a different social media management tool called Buffer app (**https://bufferapp.com/**), where you can stipulate times for your messages. You simply put your Tweets into a big Buffer bucket, and they will ping out to your network at the four times that you have pre-selected.

3 Bulk uploads

The bulk upload feature is only available to those that have a Hootsuite Pro account. Hootsuite gives you a Microsoft Excel template to complete your posts, and then you import this as a CSV file into Hootsuite. It is a bit fiddly and quite time consuming, but once you have the hang of it, you can use the same posts time and time again.

Many applications

Hootsuite also integrates with over 80 third party applications, such as RSS feeders, YouTube, MailChimp, Instagram to name a few.

The Hootsuite App Directory is a collection of extensions and applications that Hootsuite users can add to their dashboard to create a customized experience. These apps are built and maintained by third party developers and companies expanding the social content ecosystem of the Hootsuite dashboard.

Hootsuite is just one social media management tool. Here are a few others that are worth exploring:

Bufferapp.com

Buffer is a smart and easy way to schedule content across social media. Think of Buffer like a virtual queue you can use to fill with content and then stagger posting times throughout the day. This lets you keep to a consistent social media schedule all week long without worrying about micro-managing the delivery times.

SocialOomph.com

SocialOomph is a web tool that provides a host of free and paid productivity enhancements for social media. There are lots of useful Twitter features like scheduling Tweets, tracking keyword, viewing mentions and re-Tweets, DM (direct message) inbox clean up, auto-follow and auto-DM features for new followers.

Tweetdeck.com

Some of the features of Tweetdeck have changed since Twitter bought it. However, it is still an excellent social media management tool that has tons of excellent features.

Do you manage your Twitter account using a social media management tool? If "yes", then give yourself a tick in the checklist at the end of this chapter.

The Bufferapp also provides analytics about the engagement and reach of your post.

Some of the social media gurus such as Social Media Examiner use the functionality of SocialOomph, so it is well worth consideration.

Do not use the auto DM feature on SocialOomph for when someone follows you. It is impersonal and not a good Twitter strategy.

Content and engagement strategies

It is easy to become distracted when engaging in Twitter each day. Assuming Twitter is your primary social media tool, if you have the time, you should allocate approximately 30 mins of your day to seven key tasks to achieve on Twitter. Then, if you have enough time in your day then feel free to explore other areas.

Hot tip

If your target market is very active on Twitter, then allocate a minimum of 30 minutes a day to your Twitter activities. (This is an ideal scenerio – you'll be a better judge of the time you can spend on this exercise based on your other business activities.)

Use Twitter lists and start talking to people

If you are using Twitter to simply broadcast your products, services, properties or jobs then Twitter will not be a successful platform for you. Twitter is becoming a news facility to instantly receive information on industries and breaking headlines, but in reality, if you are a small business owner then the top of your list should be "engage with your target market". Set up Twitter lists (see pages 136-140 for how to set up a Twitter list).

For example, if your target market is those businesses linked to the Recruitment world, you could have a list called "Recruitment". If you can only allocate 30 minutes a day to your Twitter activities, then your Recruitment list is where you need to start. You can click on your list then re-Tweet, share, mention, communicate with the Twitter users that are in this list.

Block out the noise

There is a fantastic smartphone application called Tweetbot, which has a mute section and is extremely handy when you need to focus on pure conversation. You can launch Tweetbot when you want to talk to people who are Tweeting real live information, not automated or scheduled posts.

To give you an idea, here is a quick list of keywords or platforms that I have muted:

- #ff – as most Follow Fridays are scheduled
- #job – as I follow lots of recruiters but I am not interested in a new job
- Interesting article – as this word is also associated with scheduled Tweets
- Interesting blog
- Blog archive
- Thanks for the follow
- Worth a read
- Buffer – as all these Tweets are automated and not live
- Facebook – if a post is coming from Facebook, then I know that the person is not present on Twitter
- Paper.li – an automated newspaper service
- Scoop.it
- SocialOomph

It takes a while to figure out which keywords are worthy of being muted, but it's a great function that cuts out an awful lot of Twitter noise.

Tweet what you are up to today

Are you going to an event, perhaps meeting a client or supplier? Perhaps you are having a new kitchen fitted, or you are writing chapter four of your novel. Whatever you are doing today then schedule your Tweets throughout the day. Remember to @ mention people or companies in the posts to maximize your efforts. Be real, be authentic. Add the human touch to your Tweets and watch that interaction rise.

Schedule something from your RSS feeds or LinkedIn Pulse

You could use the RSS feeds in Hootsuite called the Hootsuite Syndicator. You can have top articles fed into your Hootsuite and then choose what to share. You can see on the next screenshot a selection of RSS feeds that I look at every day from the top social media gurus, and share articles of interest to my audience.

...cont'd

Use the Hootsuite Syndicator Application to retrieve your RSS feeds for valuable relevant content that you can share with your audience.

LinkedIn Pulse is a great source for content articles.

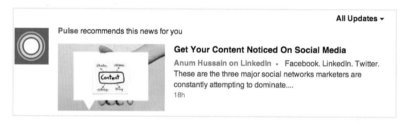

The other source of valuable content can be found on LinkedIn called Pulse (its previous name was LinkedIn Today). Simply log into LinkedIn, then click **Home** and **Pulse**. Make sure that you have customized your news beforehand. This area is covered in more detail in the LinkedIn chapter (see pages 166-200).

Congratulate people on birthdays and new jobs

If you are ahead of the game then you will already be using the LinkedIn contacts facility to find out who in your network has a birthday, a work anniversary, moved locations, etc. We suggest taking this activity one step further by clicking on the profile to see if the person has a Twitter account, or if the company has a Twitter account. Then congratulate the individuals on Twitter if their account is an active one. You may think this is time consuming, but because it is very specific, you will get more followers on Twitter and you will also enhance your relationship with the company or person. Very few people actually do this on Twitter. (Don't worry; this is fully illustrated in Chapter 6 – LinkedIn.)

Check what is trending today

"Trendjacking" otherwise known as "newsjacking", is simply the act of capitalizing on an existing trend in order to boost your own brand in the marketplace. The outcome depends on how the message lands in the view of the audience, so you have to be really careful how you use it.

If we take something that is trending such as #RoyalBabyBirth and offer our congratulations on our Facebook page or Twitter feed, then we know it is a hot topic as the world is talking about it. So putting a picture of the Royal Baby or happy couple, and asking a question, "What name do you think they will choose?", is likely to get interaction and engagement on the day that it was trending. If we did a similar post three days later, it would not have the same effect.

To find out what is trending on Twitter:

Post trending news actually on the day that it is trending. Do not autoschedule the posts, as it will dilute the impact of the Tweet.

1 Click **Home**

2 Scroll down to **Trends** (below Who to follow)

United Kingdom Trends · Change

#InterviewPalestinians
#2014powerlifting
#AFCvBEN
#MTN8
#CongratulationsMrAndMrsJones
Danny Boy
Ocampos
Paul George
Paddy Barnes
Steven Taylor

Did you know that you can change the trending results? The default is "global". However, you can change yours to your own country.

1 Click **Change**

2 Click **Change** again

...cont'd

Trends tailored just for you.

Trends offer a unique way to get closer to what you care about. They are tailored for you based on your location and who you follow.

Change | **Keep tailored Trends**

 Start typing the relevant country, then select from the dropdown menu

4 Click **Done**

> uni
>
> If you want to stop s | United Kingdom (All cities)
>
> **Nearby Locati** | United Arab Emirates (All cities)
>
> Coventry | United States (All cities)
>
> London | Nottingham | Derby
>
> Stoke-on-Trent | Bristol | Sheffield
>
> Portsmouth
>
> **Get tailored Trends** | Done

Following people

Rather than using the standard Twitter search to find users, there are two tools that you may find helpful as an alternative:

Followerwonk

www.followerwonk.com has many functions, but "search Twitter bios" is most useful. If you are looking for "Black Cab Drivers" in the City of London, then this software will show you all those that have these keywords in their Twitter bio.

...cont'd

Once you have defined your ideal target market, then sourcing them on Twitter using this free software is easy.

Twitter Advanced Search

Visit **www.Twitter.com/search-advanced** to do a more detailed Twitter search. This is a better tool to discover conversations online.

Experiment with Followerwonk to search for your key target audience Twitterers, by searching Twitter bios.

159

Advanced **Search**

Words

All of these words

This exact phrase

Any of these words

None of these words

These hashtags

Written in   Any Language

People

From these accounts

To these accounts

Mentioning these accounts

Places

Near this place

Other

Select   Positive) Negative (Question ? Include retweets

Search

Cleanse your account each month

It is important to make sure that you cleanse your account each month, by unfollowing people who have not Tweeted in the last six months, or perhaps clearing out some of those Twitterers that you are following who are "egg heads" (see page 160) and have not branded their accounts. A good tool that assists you in the monthly cleansing of your account is **www.manageflitter.com**

Once a month, unfollow any Twitter accounts that are inactive or fake.

Who is following you?

Did you know that there are millions of fake accounts out there (called Tweetbots), that are randomly following people for no reason whatsoever? It is suggested that there are over 20 million Tweetbots in the Twittersphere.

Twitter is certainly cracking down on these accounts, but it is interesting to see if any of your followers, or your competitors' followers are fake.

Check online using fake.statuspeople.com
This site has a basic free package, and limited searches, but it has a unique algorithm that tells you how many Twitter followers are fake, inactive or engaged within a matter of seconds.

ManageFlitter produces similar results. However, this particular software seems to be more accurate.

Here are some ways to spot a fake profile, so you do not waste your time following them in the first place:

Are they an Egg Head?

The default Twitter avatar is an egg head. If you are following someone who is an "egg head" this can be a sure sign that they are a fake profile or a Tweetbot. Not all egg heads are fake. However, if the Twitter user has not even bothered to change their profile picture then surely you must question if they are actually worthy of a follow?

They very rarely have a Twitter bio
If the Twitter bio is completely empty, with no link to a website, then it is usually a sure giveaway that this is a fake account.

They publish incoherent Tweets

Yes, Tweets that makes absolutely no sense whatsoever! Gobbledegook messages that are completely random. Or the alternative is that they publish duplicate content with a link, time and time again and may tag in specific users.

When did they last Tweet?

If their last Tweet was three years ago, then why are they starting to follow you, or why would you consider following them? If they are following you, but have not Tweeted in a long time, then this is a sure sign that they are a fake account.

Do they have 2001 followers?

Twitter has a rule that you cannot follow more than 2000 people if you do not have 2000 people following you. (Go Twitter! This is an excellent rule!). You will often spot the fake profiles as they are following 2001 people and they need to wait until they get 2000 followers before they can increase their numbers. I wonder how many dormant Twitter accounts are hovering around the Twittersphere that are stuck at 2001?

What is your fake score? If you have more than 10% fake then this is something that you need to have a look at and do some culling and it is time to give your Twitter account a bit of a cleanse. If you are under 10% then congratulations, you deserve a tick in the box in the checklist at the end of this chapter.

Conclusion

1 Build your platform

Have you built your Twitter account correctly? Have you branded your background skin to showcase your services and contact details? Have you included a header and an avatar that works well in the timeline? Have you registered your accounts on the Twitter directories? Have you set up your Twitter lists? If you can answer "yes" to all of the above, then congratulations, you have reached stage one of Twitter success for the small business owner.

2 Grow your network

What is your follower/following ratio? Is it a healthy ratio? Are you using Followerwonk or an alternative to regularly follow new people? Are you using the invitation function in Twitter to email your network? Are you cleansing your account each month? Are you implementing a "notice me" strategy to grow those important prospect clients? Do you have Twitter lists set up that you are focusing on each day? If you can confidently say that you are doing everything in your power to grow your network on Twitter, then congratulations, you have reached stage two of Twitter success for the small business owner.

3 Implement a strategy

Are you writing your 20% broadcasting Tweets and scheduling those in a social media dashboard such as Hootsuite or Bufferapp.com? Have you defined your target market and created specific lists in Twitter to engage with them? Are you following press or industry-specific Twitter accounts to enable you to share content? Have you set up your RSS feeds so that you do not miss any valuable content which your audience may be interested in? Have you decided how much time you are going to be spending on Twitter each day? Do you know when your network is online the most so you know when to Tweet your most important Tweets to have the best impact? What is your strategy for Follow Fridays? What is your listening strategy?

If you feel that you are organized, and you have set your goals and objectives for Twitter, and you have considered the majority of the above questions, then congratulations, you are en route to a successful Twitter account.

4 Measure the results

The same as all marketing, it is important to measure your results, otherwise how do you know if you are being successful? Since Twitter is very open, there is a vast number of statistics that you can measure, but the key is to make sure that you are heading in the right direction and communicating with your audience to achieve your set goals and objectives.

For example, your main objective may be to "drive traffic to my website". If so, then the key measurement will come from your Google Analytics and the social source traffic. However, if your key objective is "customer retention", then you should be measuring the @mentions and conversational goals that your business is having online.

If you are using a social media management tool such as Hootsuite, TweetDeck, SocialOomph, SproutSocial, etc., then they all offer statistics for your Twitter account. The object of running these reports is to learn from them, tweak your strategy and try to increase the numbers the following month.

Checklist

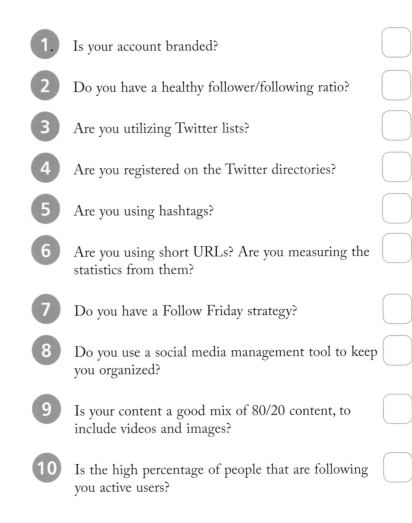

1. Is your account branded?

2 Do you have a healthy follower/following ratio?

3 Are you utilizing Twitter lists?

4 Are you registered on the Twitter directories?

5 Are you using hashtags?

6 Are you using short URLs? Are you measuring the statistics from them?

7 Do you have a Follow Friday strategy?

8 Do you use a social media management tool to keep you organized?

9 Is your content a good mix of 80/20 content, to include videos and images?

10 Is the high percentage of people that are following you active users?

6 LinkedIn

An introduction to LinkedIn

LinkedIn is recognized more as a professional social networking site. If your target market is business-to-business, rather than business-to-consumer, then having a professional LinkedIn presence is a must. Some people feel that LinkedIn is becoming a place where job seekers and recruiters hangout, but it is so much more than that. Here are key reasons to use LinkedIn for your business:

● A great place to engage with and attract new potential clients

● An excellent tool to source reliable suppliers

● The ability to maintain "Top Of Mind Awareness"

● One of the best and effective ways to recruit new staff

● The capacity to drive traffic to your website

● The capacity to promote your products and services

● The possibility of using it as a hub to collect testimonials and recommendations

● The power to learn new skills and to be kept informed of industry news

● The advantage of monitoring your competition

● Great resource for gaining answers to tough business questions quickly

● To promote customer retention and to nurture those existing client relationships

Before you can set up your business or company page you need to set up your personal profile if you don't have one. If you already have this in place ensure it is up-to-date.

21 steps to your personal LinkedIn profile

First, you need to make sure your personal profile is completed correctly.

Click **Profile** and then **Edit Profile**

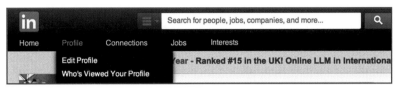

1 **Your name**

Your name should only display your actual name. It is against LinkedIn rules to add telephone numbers, email addresses, symbols, or even LION (LinkedIn Open Networker) after your name. LinkedIn is becoming quite strict with this rule and you will soon see these disappearing.

To change your name, simply click the pencil next to your name.

2 **Your professional headline**

The default for your professional headline is your job title and company name. However, your professional headline is indexed by LinkedIn and also search engines. Therefore, it is recommended to change your headline to display keywords within your industry.

To change your professional headline, click the pencil.

You will not be able to set up a company page on LinkedIn without having a personal profile first. Register at www. linkedin.com

LION is an acronym for LinkedIn Open Networker. LIONs are LinkedIn members who are open to networking with everyone, irrespective of whether they know the people who have asked them to connect or not. The LION generally accepts every invitation request to connect or, at least, will not click the "I Don't Know" button in response to an invitation.

Adding telephone numbers after your name is against LinkedIn rules and will eventually be deleted by LinkedIn.

...cont'd

Your name should ONLY include your name. No numbers, no sales pitch, no LION

Your headline should be catchy and have keywords you would like to be found for

Your photo should always look professional

Connections

3 Your avatar/profile picture

Refrain from adding a company logo, as this should be saved for your company LinkedIn page and not your personal profile. A professional head and shoulders image is ideal.

To add or change your profile picture click the camera icon. With a maximum file size of 4MB, you can upload a square JPG, GIF or PNG. The default size of a LinkedIn avatar on your profile page is 200 x 200 pixels, but you can click to enlarge the image up to 450 x 450 pixels.

4 Connections

Your first goal should be to reach at least 501 connections for social proof, verification and excellent networking opportunities. When you are searching for contacts in the advanced search area, the results shown are the results from your network. If you have a larger network, then you automatically have better search results. (How to connect with people is shown later on page 184.) If "search" is not an important factor for your reason to be on LinkedIn, then you may argue that quality is better than quantity, and I would agree with this.

5 Add relevant contact information

This will include showcasing your company email. If you have set up your LinkedIn account with a Gmail/Hotmail/AOL etc. email, then that is fine, but you should add your company email to your LinkedIn account and make this the primary email which is displayed on your profile. Add additional information such as your Skype name.

Click **Edit Profile**

Edit your email address if necessary

Add your password to the field to access your private settings

Linked in

```
julia.doherty@green-umbrella.biz

Password                              ?

            Sign In
```

Add your company email address, and select **Make Primary**

You can see from the example on the next page that I have three email addresses on my LinkedIn account. I can log in to LinkedIn with any of these emails. However, I only showcase my company email.

An email must be verified before you can make it into a primary email. LinkedIn will email you a link, which you simply click to verify that the address exists.

...cont'd

You are allowed to add up to three websites on your LinkedIn company profile. It is highly recommended that you label your websites rather than selecting "Company Website".

For example, rather than showcasing websites to read like this:

In this example, the default settings in LinkedIn are used, which doesn't indicate where the "Company Website" links will take you

170

It is much more intuitive for the reader if you label your websites correctly so that they look more like this:

Now that the websites have been labeled, your visitors can see instantly where the destination website will be

To label your websites: Click the pencil > Click **Other** > Give your website a label > Click **Save**

Hot tip

Always label your websites correctly for maximum impact.

Edit your profile URL

Your original profile website address (URL) will be a mix of names and numbers and be unmemorable. To ensure that you have a clean-looking URL, which needs to be your name rather than a company name:

Click **Edit** next to your current URL

in uk.linkedin.com/in/juliadoherty/   Edit

Then click Customize your public profile URL

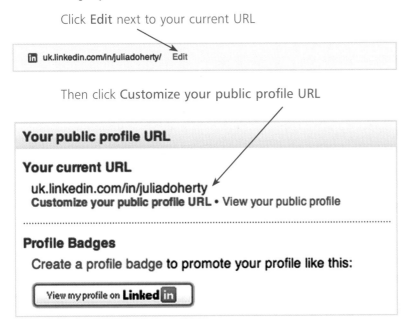

Your public profile URL

Your current URL

uk.linkedin.com/in/juliadoherty
Customize your public profile URL • View your public profile

Profile Badges

Create a profile badge to promote your profile like this:

View my profile on **Linked** in

Finally, type in a relevant username, which should be your name, or a variation of your name, and not a company name. Once this is set, it is set for life and cannot be altered, so choose wisely.

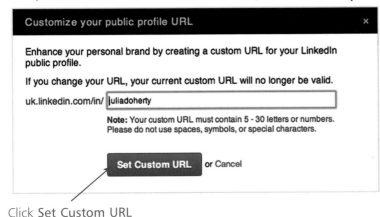

Customize your public profile URL   ×

Enhance your personal brand by creating a custom URL for your LinkedIn public profile.

If you change your URL, your current custom URL will no longer be valid.

uk.linkedin.com/in/ |juliadoherty

Note: Your custom URL must contain 5 - 30 letters or numbers.
Please do not use spaces, symbols, or special characters.

Set Custom URL   or Cancel

Click **Set Custom URL**

Don't forget

You can only edit your profile URL once. Therefore, make sure it is your name, rather than a company name.

...cont'd

Add ALL relevant contact information

Customize your website addresses with terms that attract your target market, rather than "Company Website"

Edit your profile URL and get rid of those horrible numbers

Hot tip

Posting regularly is essential.

8 Regularly update your activity

To stay in the minds of your clients and connections on LinkedIn, it is important to share regular content. Bear in mind that this is very much a business and professional network, so announcing to the world what you are having for breakfast today is not really something that you would share on this platform. Posting between 1-5 times a day seems to be an optimum number to have the most effect on a LinkedIn personal profile.

What kind of updates should you share on LinkedIn?
Here is a list of suggestions that may inspire you:

- Sharing a valuable article from LinkedIn Pulse (see page 197)
- Conversations that you may want to start
- Information about an event you or your company are attending
- Posting your blog articles
- Posting your audio and video links
- Announcing the networking event that you are attending and tagging in an individual or company that you are expecting to meet there
- Adding tips or techniques about your industry or trade
- Giving your opinion on trending topics or news headlines
- Sharing content from your RSS feeds

...cont'd

- Sharing your connections' content that may be relevant to your audience

Sharing an activity update on LinkedIn:

Click **Home**

Click in the box and type your message here to **Share an update...**

Add the URL to your post. Once the URL has been imported below, you can delete the URL from your update

The link below it will remain

Click here to edit the title and the content

9 **Use keywords in your summary**

The summary of your profile is highly indexed by LinkedIn and search engines such as Google. Therefore, it is important to make sure that you have specific keywords within your summary.

There are many variations of summaries on LinkedIn profiles and there really is no right or wrong way. Keynotes are:

- Do not make it too long (no more than five paragraphs)
- Add those keywords
- Write in the first person

Hot tip

Do not write more than five paragraphs in your LinkedIn profile summary.

174

10 **Write in the first person**

This is your profile, which is written by you! Therefore, it does not read correctly if you have not written it as the first person. This is sometimes difficult to do, but your summary needs to read in an authentic light, perhaps upselling key features of your business in the middle, and then showcasing some of your main achievements at the end.

11 **Add rich text media to your profile**

Adding rich text media, or more commonly known as visuals, such as videos, PDFs, PowerPoint presentations, links etc. to various parts of your LinkedIn profile is essential and will take your profile to another level.

These areas are:

- Your summary
- Experience (employment history)
- Education

Click the pencil to edit your summary

Click the square + icon to add rich text media

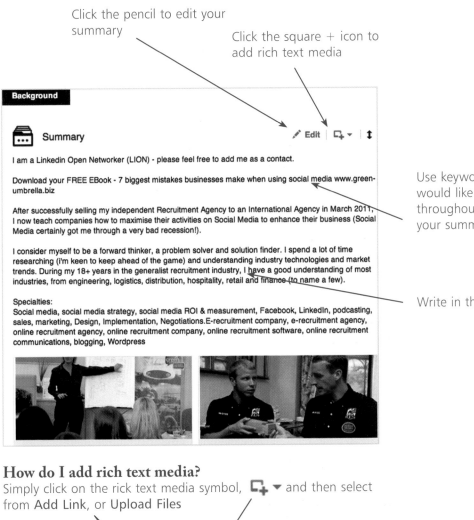

Use keywords that you would like to be found throughout the whole of your summary

Write in the first person

How do I add rich text media?

Simply click on the rick text media symbol, and then select from **Add Link**, or **Upload Files**

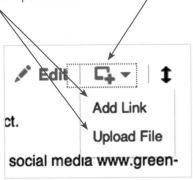

...cont'd

In the example below, I have clicked on **Add a link.** You can only add links from the list of supported providers. (However there are lots of providers, and the list is increasing each month). The two main providers are YouTube and SlideShare.

Some ideas that you may want to add as rich text media files are:

- A company brochure
- An eBook
- A PowerPoint or SlideShare presentation about your company
- A company promotional video
- A white paper
- Fact sheets

12 **Clear calls to action**

Once you have uploaded your rich text media then add clear calls to action on each caption.

Make sure you give clear instructions to your audience, e.g. Join, Click here, etc.

...cont'd

13 Make the most of your skills and endorsements

Take a few minutes to make sure that your skills are listed correctly on your profile. If you do not yet have any endorsements on your key skills then you can move them around so that the most important ones appear at the top of your list. (Just drag and drop).

Click the pencil to edit your skills

Start typing a relevant skill and then select from the dropdown menu

Skills & Endorsements ✎ Edit | ↕

Skills and Endorsements Settings ❓

I want to be endorsed ⦿ Yes ○ No

☑ Include me in endorsement suggestions to my connections
☑ Show me suggestions to endorse my connections
☑ Send me notifications via email when my connections endorse me

Add & Remove ❓ | **Manage Endorsements** ❓

social| **Add**

Social **Media**
Social **Media Marketing**   × 99+ Facebook ×
Social **Networking**   g × 95 Email Marketing ×
Social **Services**   Marketing × 46 YouTube ×
Corporate Social **Responsibility**   34 LinkedIn ×
Social **Skills**   witter × 35 Advertising ×
Social **Entrepreneurship**   Recruitment Advertising ×
Social **Marketing**   6 Pinterest × 12 Podcasting ×
Social **Sciences**

Keyword your skills that you want to be endorsed for. Make sure the most important ones are at the top!

177

Hot tip

If your skillset has not appeared in the dropdown menu then simply click **Add** and it will create a new skill that others can also select in the future.

...cont'd

When you receive a notification that someone has endorsed you for a skill, then make sure that you take the time to thank him or her in a message. Keep conversation and dialogue flowing on LinkedIn as this is the key to success.

Hover over the latest endorsement and Click **Send a message** to the person to thank them for endorsing you

Always thank people for endorsing you.

14 Update your Projects

If you have not yet added projects to your profile, they can be found on the right-hand side, alongside certificates, languages, test scores, etc.

Use the projects section to highlight any free reports, downloads or to showcase any products that you are promoting.

A project can be used for many ideas. If you have resources such as white papers, brochures, case studies, etc. that people can download or link to then this area is incredibly useful.

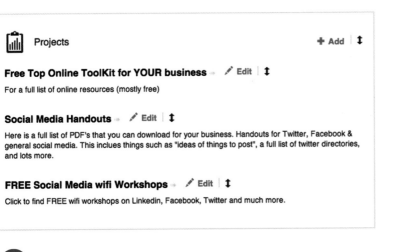

Only place items here that offer some value to your audience. Do not over sell!

15 Experience

Once again, your job title is indexed and appears on search engines. If you are a director of a company, then type **Director** but add some keywords about your business.

To edit your existing role click **Edit**

To add a new role click + **Add a position**

Start typing the name of your company and select from the dropdown menu. Once you have selected your company, completed the relevant fields and clicked save, the logo of the business will appear on your profile.

You may have more than one current job. The icon on the right hand side (as shown in this screen shot) enables you to reposition the role so that your most important job is at the top.

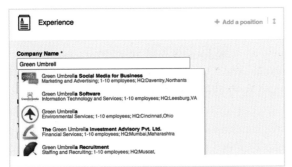

...cont'd

If the logo is not on your profile it signifies that the company was not selected from the dropdown menu, or that the owners of that page have not added the logo to the company page.

16 Job Description

Your job description will ideally be between 3-4 short paragraphs, which have keyword-rich content. As you will see from the job description below, numerous keywords have been added that are relevant to the industry, such as "social media", "recruitment", "Facebook", "LinkedIn", "Blogging" etc. What keywords are relevant in your industry?

Add keywords in your job title

Add keywords within the job description. It will be picked up by Google!

17 Recommendations

Make it part of your process to request a recommendation on your LinkedIn profile.

To request a recommendation, click **Profile** and then select the dropdown arrow next to **Edit profile**

Don't forget

You can only ask for a recommendation from LinkedIn members that are connected to you.

There is a limit of 200 recipients of a recommendation request that can be sent at any one time. It is worth noting that if you are requesting recommendations in bulk then the email that arrives in the recipient's inbox will not be a group email; they are sent individually by LinkedIn.

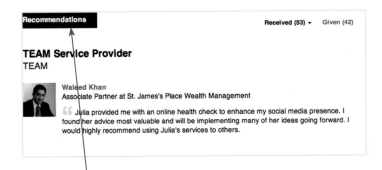

You can send bulk recommendation requests. The recipients will not see other email addresses.

Recommendations are extremely important! Try to have at least 10. If you have less than 10, then make it your top mission!

Advice for contacting

This area of your profile is on public view. Visitors to your profile will only be able to see the contact information of your profile if you are a first connection. However, if you add your contact information to this area of your profile, then anyone will be able to contact you, depending on which information you select to advertise.

This area can be found towards the bottom of your LinkedIn profile.

Honors and Awards

Are you accredited with a governing body? Have you, or your business, won any awards? If so, then these may added here.

Limit how many groups to join

LinkedIn has capped the number of groups that you can join to 50. In any case, if you are actively involved in 50 groups each day then you will have very little time to run your business. Limit your groups and only spend time in the groups that are active and that you feel have some value, otherwise you may be wasting your valuable time and energy.

What are groups?
LinkedIn call them "Interest Groups" and as of August 2014,

...cont'd

there are currently 2,018,719 groups. To find the LinkedIn Groups directory visit **https://linkedin.com/vsearch/ g?orig=GLHD**

Groups were formed to create an area for discussion of a particular industry or topic and they are extremely popular on LinkedIn.

Groups can be closed and accessible to members only, or they can be open for anyone to join. Managing an active group can be quite time consuming, so take this into consideration if you are about to embark on that journey.

To join a group, click **Interests** on the homepage and then select **Groups**

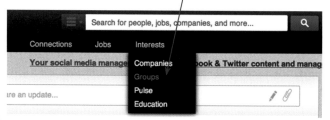

Simply search for the keywords or the topic that you are interested in and click **Join**

21 **Showcase your groups on your profile**

On your personal profile, it is important to showcase the key groups. You can change the order in which they appear on your page in the LinkedIn settings of your personal profile.

Click the **Groups, Companies & Applications** tab in settings, then click **Select your group display order**

Hot tip

Do not sell or broadcast your company messages within a group. To be successful you can add value by creating good topics of discussion.

...cont'd

From here you can decide which order your groups can be displayed on your profile.

Make sure that your own groups are showcased in the top five on your profile (this is changed in the settings area)

Groups (5)

Order	Group Name	
1	TEAM - The Employment Agents Movement	Member Settings
2 ⇅	Heart Of Business	Manager Settings | Member Settings
3 ⇅	Customer Services Management Professionals	Member Settings
4 ⇅	Milton Keynes Networkers	Member Settings
5 ⇅	Recruiter magazine	Member Settings

[Save Changes] or Cancel

Groups

 CSM
Customer Services M...
Visible ›

 HEART
Heart Of Business
Visible ›

 MK Networkers
Milton Keynes Netwo...
Hidden ›

Recruiter
Recruiter magazine
Visible ›

 TEAM
TEAM - The Employ...
Visible ›

 Hot tip

Update your profile at least once every three months. It is amazing how things change. Put a date in your diary to remind you.

Connecting with people

You can ask people to connect with you on LinkedIn by sending them a personal invitation. Once they accept this invitation they will be come a 1st degree connection, and you will see a little "1st" in the top right-hand corner of their profile. If you see a "2nd" or "3rd", then this tells you that you are not yet connected.

You can invite people to connect with you from a variety of sources:

- **The People You May Know page**
- **The Add Connections page** (you can search your email address book to find contacts, or even import data from your CRM system into LinkedIn)
- **A member's profile** (simply click the Connect button on their profile)
- **Search results** (click connect to the right of the person's information)

To send out an invitation:

 Choose **How do you know this person?** If none of the options are relevant to the person that you wish to connect with then you could join one of the groups that person is a member of first.

 Personalize your invitation to connect by deleting the pre-populated email and replacing it with something more specific. By doing this you will increase your changes of being accepted.

Beware

LinkedIn affords each member a lifetime supply of 3,000 invitations, so use your invitations sparingly. If you have reached your limit then you can request additional invitations by clicking on the Contact Us button and asking LinkedIn to increase your limit. However, this is not guaranteed.

Hot tip

If you have met people on other platforms, or perhaps at a networking event, conference or even in the local pub, then ask them to connect with you online.

Don't forget

You can't paste any website address links or attachments into your invitation.

LinkedIn company page

There are many reasons why you should have a company LinkedIn page, but here are four key benefits:

- LinkedIn company pages are found by Google and highly indexed on LinkedIn.

- Providing a professional presence on one of the largest business networking sites.

- A great place to showcase the talents and skills of your team. This could be a freelancer who is happy to be associated with your business on LinkedIn, your co-directors and staff.

- A place to showcase your company news, achievements and successes.

Set up a company LinkedIn page

LinkedIn is sophisticated and will only allow one company profile to be created per domain name. In addition to this, you must have a domain name email within your profile settings to enable you to create the page.

This eliminates any duplication of pages within LinkedIn.

Example – if you wanted to create a LinkedIn company page for "Joe Blogs Software":

● Joe Blogs must have a website – e.g. www.joeblogssoftware.co.uk

● On your personal profile, you must have a domain name email address for the same company, i.e. joe@joeblogssoftware.co.uk

● If you do not have an email address that matches the website, then you will be unable to set up your company page on LinkedIn

To set up a LinkedIn page for your company, follow these steps:

 Click **Interests** and then click **Companies** in the dropdown menu

Create a Company Page

Raise brand awareness, announce career opportunities, and promote your products and services with a LinkedIn Company Page.

Learn More ▸

Create

 On the far right hand side of the page, click **Create**

3 Complete the basic details required, tick the verification box and then click **Continue**

Add a Company

Company Pages offer public information about each company on LinkedIn. To add a Company Page, please enter the company name and your email address at this company. Only current employees are eligible to create a Company Page.

Company name:

Your email address at company:

☐ I verify that I am the official representative of this company and have the right to act on behalf of my company in the creation of this page.

Continue or Cancel

Once you have a basic page completed, here is a full checklist of everything else needed on your page:

How does your LinkedIn Company Page score in the 5-point check below?

1 **Does your business page have an overview banner?**

With exception to the avatar (company logo), the overview banner is the first impression that you give of your company LinkedIn page. It is important to make sure that this image is consistent in brand, and looks professional.

Overview Banner: Minimum 646 x 220 pixels, PNG/JPEG/GIF format, maximum size of file is 2MB.

Avatar/Company Logo: 100 x 60 pixels, PNG/JPEG/GIF format, maximum size of file is 2MB.

...cont'd

Avatar

Overview

How do I add an avatar and overview banner?

Click **Edit page**

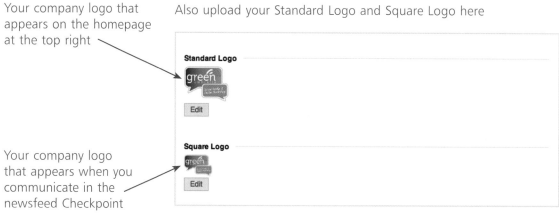

Scroll down until you reach the Image area and click **Edit** for each image and upload your images

Your company logo that appears on the homepage at the top right

Also upload your Standard Logo and Square Logo here

Your company logo that appears when you communicate in the newsfeed Checkpoint

2 ## Have you completed your company description?

- The company name and description is picked up by search engines. Therefore, a full and complete company description is essential.
- LinkedIn allows a maximum of 2,000 characters to be added to your company page description, which is ample content.

To edit your company page summary

Click Edit > Edit page

Add or edit your company details

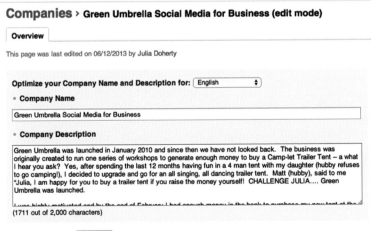

Ensure that your company description is complete and make the most of your 2,000 character allowance with keyword rich content.

...cont'd

3 Content techniques for LinkedIn pages

Content that is customized to the followers of your page and your customers' professional interests certainly works best.

When posting an update, use concise introductions and eye-catching headlines. Make your content short. It needs to be appealing so that others will share the content with their connections. One of the easiest ways to encourage engagement is by adding an image, video or a link. If you do not have any of these to share, then consider asking questions that are relevant to your industry. For example, "How often do you post on LinkedIn?"

There are various techniques to learn when posting an activity update on LinkedIn.

How do you add a status update?

Click in the Update status area and type a standard text update

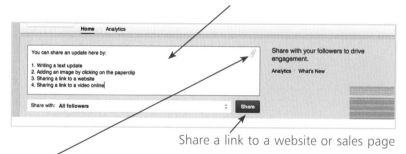

Share a link to a website or sales page

Add an image, by clicking the small paperclip on the right. Adding images to your company page updates can be a highly effective way to get engagement on your page

Hot tip

Always add a little "Update to" in the main update box to explain why you are sharing this particular link, or to give a call to action.

...cont'd

There are some recommended techniques when adding a link to a status update within your company page illustrated below:

- Copy and paste the URL (website address) from your original source. Once the details have been imported you can delete the website address from the update. This gives the update a cleaner look.

- This whole area is editable. If you want to amend the title or any other text, simply click on the fields for the title and the description becomes editable.

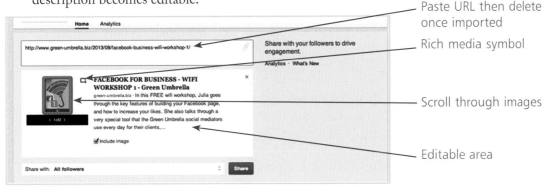

Paste URL then delete once imported

Rich media symbol

Scroll through images

Editable area

- You have two ways of changing the default image that LinkedIn have selected for you. Simply scroll through the number of images that LinkedIn has imported from the website address, or click on the rich media symbol and add your own image.

Keep in mind that LinkedIn users will be checking your updates on multiple devices, so ensure that you are mixing your content on a regular basis.

Do all employees have their accounts linked to your page?

If you have a number of people in your team then suggest they link their profiles to your company page. LinkedIn company pages were only introduced a few years ago. Therefore, if your employees were early users of LinkedIn then they may not have your company page linked to their personal profile.

...cont'd

If you are the owner of the business, then you may want to first take a look to see how many employees have linked their profile to your company page.

Click on **Home**, then on the far right, click **See all**

If you have some staff missing from this page, then you can ask them if they would like to link their profiles to the page.

How do I link a personal profile to a company page?

 Return to **Edit profile**.

2 Scroll down to the experience area and then click **Edit** next to the area where you typed your company name. If you have a logo on the far right then this signifies that your company page is already linked. If not, then you need to go to Step 3.

Click **Change Company**

Company Name *
Green Umbrella Social Media for Business Change Company | Edit Display Name
Title *
Digital Marketing and Social Media Agency Owner
Location
Northants
Time Period *
November ⬍ | 2009 | – Present
☑ I currently work here

Start typing your company name and then select your company from the dropdown menu

Don't forget

Select your company from the dropdown menu.

Click **Save**

5   **Have you linked your featured groups?**

If you are an administrator of a group on LinkedIn and it has some relevance to your company page, then you can showcase the group on your homepage.

To add a featured group to your company page

Click on **Edit page**

Scroll down to the **Featured Groups** area. You can showcase up to three featured groups on your company page

Simply start typing the name of your group, then select from the dropdown menu

Beware

You can only feature a group on your company page if you are an administrator of the group.

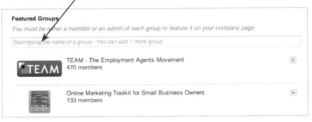

What are Showcase Pages?

In April 2014, LinkedIn decided to remove the products and services page that was associated with a LinkedIn company page. This has been replaced by Showcase Pages.

A Showcase Page is featured on your company page in the sidebar. As you can see in the example below, Adobe has a main page, but it also has sister companies that are associated with the main organization. These can now be linked in one place with Showcase Pages.

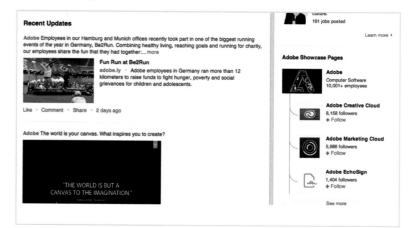

Here are some considerations before you create a Showcase Page for all of your products, services, sectors, branches, etc:

- You will need to provide content for each of your Showcase Pages if you wish your page to be found.
- There will also be the additional cost of branding each page with a "hero" image.
- If you have a part of your business that reflects a unique target audience, then consider setting up a Showcase Page for that particular product or service. But do not set up a Showcase Page to the detriment of your main page; it will dilute your message.

For example:

Green Umbrella is a digital marketing agency, but specializes in a niche market for the recruitment industry. It makes sense to have a Showcase Page just for "Social Media for Recruiters", as those who are following the main company page will have no interest in posts about online marketing for this specific niche.

However, there is no point in setting up a Showcase Page for "General Marketing Services", as this content would be valuable to everyone who is following the main company page, and not just email marketing.

The key message here is to create Showcase Pages where you have a particular target market, with targeted content for that niche.

Create a Showcase Page

To create a Showcase Page:

 From the main company page click **Edit** and select **Create a Showcase Page** from the dropdown menu

 Give your new page a name. Showcase Page names are unique and, therefore, there are limited domains. For example, it will be highly unlikely that you can call the page "Roofing Products" if you are a roofer, as this name may have already been taken

 Give your page an overview banner (see pages 187-188). The sizes are very specific; therefore, you may need to ask your designer to create an image for you

 The description on a Showcase Page is limited to 200 characters (just a little bit bigger than a Tweet), so you may need to be creative

5 Remember to add your unique website URL to direct people to find out more information

Key day-to-day activities

To help you with some day-to-day activities on LinkedIn, here are five key activities that you can do each day, that will keep you busy for approximately 30 minutes a day, but will lead you to LinkedIn success:

 1   **Connect with people every single day**

Utilize the contacts facility (click **Connections** or download the smartphone LinkedIn app named **Connected**. Ensure that you are congratulating those who are celebrating a work anniversary, a birthday today, relocating or who have secured a new job.

In this area, you will also receive any reminder functions that you may have set for yourself.

2   **Share a popular article from LinkedIn Pulse**

Make sure that you have customized your news in LinkedIn Pulse (previously known as LinkedIn Today). Once you have clicked on the word **Pulse** from your homepage, ensure that you have customized the news articles within LinkedIn Pulse so that you are receiving articles of interest that are relevant to you and your audience.

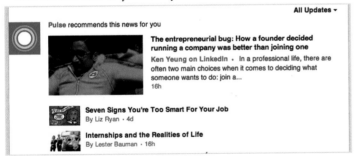

In your settings you can request that a summary of the popular articles in the categories that you have selected is emailed to you each day. Or just click on **Your News** in Pulse to get the latest articles.

Don't forget

30 minutes a day is the ideal time, but may not be practical for your business.

Hot tip

If a person has a new job, then always double check to make sure that they have not simply changed their professional headline and that they have secured a brand new position before you click on the congratulations button.

...cont'd

If you have received an endorsement, then take a minute to message the individual to say thank you. Do not feel obligated to say thank you by returning the endorsement; a simple direct message will suffice.

Groups are created for discussions; they are not there as a sales tool. Therefore, jumping into a group and posting links to your jobs, your website, or a message about your latest services or products will simply alienate the people in the group.

 Check your notifications

Each day, check your notifications to see if people have commented on a discussion, activity update or have perhaps given you an endorsement.

4 **Be active in a key group**

If your target market is present in a strong and active group on LinkedIn, then this is where you should be focusing your attention to maximize the opportunity of the time that you have allocated.

The most effective way to become known in a group is to start discussions that the members feel passionate about. If you are constantly a top contributor in the group then members (and your target market) will soon get to know and respect you for your industry knowledge.

5 **Share an update**

The bottom line is that LinkedIn is a social network. Rather than posting an array of features about your products, engage in topical conversations about everyday life. Check Twitter to see what is trending today (or visit **www.whatstrending.com**). Give your opinion on something that has happened in the news today and tag people in posts that you have met throughout the week.

Be the person whose updates everyone enjoys because they feel like they are getting to know the real you. At the end of the day, it's a cliché, but people buy from people.

Conclusion

 Build your platform
The two key areas are your LinkedIn personal profile and your company page. If you have completed the 21 steps to create your personal profile, and the 5 steps to create your LinkedIn company page, then you have reached stage one for success on LinkedIn.

 Grow your network
There are too many strategies to mention in this book. However, the key is to make sure that you are connecting with people on LinkedIn. Look at the suggestions that LinkedIn provides in the "People you may know" section.

If you have achieved your 501 connections on LinkedIn, and you have a substantial number of followers of your company LinkedIn page, then congratulations, you have achieved stage two of success on LinkedIn.

 Implement a strategy
To get started on a LinkedIn strategy you first need to define your social media goals. (See pages 17-23).

 Measure the results

The LinkedIn company page has detailed insights. However, it is difficult to measure the success of the personal profile.

To find more detailed analytics for your company page, click on **Analytics**

If you are using MS Outlook, Gmail or Yahoo! mail then check out **www.xobni.com** (inbox spelt backwards). This neat tool will attach to your email software and produce extra columns. These columns will provide you with social networking intelligence, and will give you links to the senders' LinkedIn, Facebook and Twitter accounts. If you have a smartphone, then take a look at Evernote, which enables you to connect with individuals on LinkedIn that you meet when out and about.

From here you will see a range of statistics for reach, engagement, most popular posts and a comparison with other companies that you manage

If driving traffic back to your website was one of your main objectives, then check the social traffic source on your Google Analytics statistics (covered in pages 258-260).

Checklist

How professional is your LinkedIn profile?

1 Have you included keywords within your professional headline?

2 Have you labeled your websites correctly or do they still say "Company website"?

3 Have you grabbed your unique URL?

4 Have you added your Twitter account(s)?

5 Do you have a completed summary and is it written in the first person with a full list of specialisms?

6 Have you included Rich Text Media in your profile summary? That is, have you added visuals, PDFs, slideshare presentations, videos, etc. to enhance your profile?

7 Is your profile linked to your Company Page?

8 Do you have a minimum of 10 skills listed?

9 Do you have a minimum of 10 recommendations?

10 Have you added "additional information" which is viewable to the public?

7 Pinterest

What is Pinterest?

Pinterest is a tool for collecting and organizing the things that inspire you. Millions of people are using Pinterest in their work and their daily lives. No matter what you are interested in, you will find an image of it on Pinterest.

It is also a very vibrant social networking site, but to be strictly accurate, it is actually a social bookmarking site.

Pinterest was launched in 2010 and the clue to its philosophy lies in its name. Pinterest is a virtual pin board.

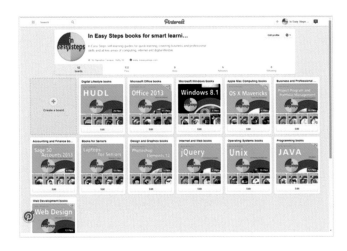

Is Pinterest important for my business?

Pinterest is amongst the top five largest social networking sites, and this should not be ignored. If your business is visual in any way, or you have an ecommerce site that sells products, a design portfolio, or if you produce regular content on your website (blogging or articles) then Pinterest will be a valuable platform for your business. Here are the five main reasons why you should consider Pinterest as part of your social media strategy:

Pinterest converts pinners into customers

The route to your website from Pinterest is just one click away (once you have pinned your image correctly).

This quote, taken from the Hubspot website sums it up.

> 66 *For retailers, the path to purchase from a social network is no more direct than on Pinterest. 'See it, like it, buy it' happens frequently. Even in cases where the path to purchase is not as direct, rarely do you have a social network where linking to for-sale items is done so frequently. You have clear social proof of the desire for the item, you can see a picture of it, and you are only one or two clicks away from being on an e-commerce site.* 99
>
> Josh Davis of LLsocial.com clearly explains the workings of Pinterest behavior

Source: http://www.devetol.com/how-and-why-to-use-pinterest-for-social-media-marketing/

Pinterest drives traffic to your website

According to a survey by Shareaholic (*https://blog.shareaholic.com/pinterest-referral-traffic/*), Pinterest is now driving more referral traffic than Google+, LinkedIn and YouTube combined. This is one reason why we recommend pinning your blogs and articles from your website.

Pinning your blog articles to Pinterest can result in fantastic referral traffic to your website.

...cont'd

Every pin can include a link back to a website. Therefore, the possibilities are endless.

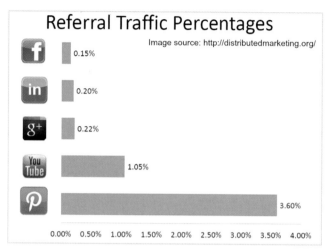

Pinterest integrates with other social networks

It is crucial that your social networking platforms can integrate with each other and Pinterest is a prime example of this.

Facebook integration works with a personal profile only. However, if you connect your personal profile to a Facebook page application called Pinvolve, then you can post pins from an allocated board straight to your Facebook business page's timeline (see page 209).

Twitter integration is also extremely smooth, and works well as you can Tweet your pins to your Twitter account by simply ticking a box whilst pinning.

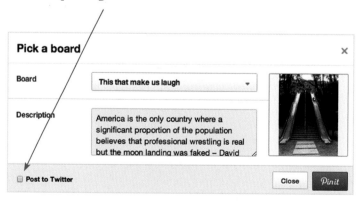

Website integration

There are lots of goodies available for website integration. Visit **http://about.pinterest.com/goodies/** to find out more.

The **Pin it** button extension makes it easy to pin anything to your pin boards from any website.

It is highly addictive

Pinterest is one of those social networking platforms which is highly addictive, and once you start pinning, you can't stop. This results in a highly engaged audience and is very powerful for business.

As Pinterest is a visual platform, it is easy to absorb information quickly, which is possibly the main reason it has become so successful.

Set up a business account

There is currently very little difference between a personal account and a business account on Pinterest. However, it is worth setting your account up correctly as they will be introducing more features on the business side over coming months and years.

There are also two sets of terms associated with Pinterest. You can find the business terms here: **http://business.pinterest.com/tos/** The personal terms are here: **http://about.pinterest.com/en/terms-service**

If you already have a personal Pinterest account that you would like to migrate into a business account, then follow these steps:

1 **Visit business.pinterest.com**
If you already have a personal Pinterest account then click **Convert here**. If you are starting from scratch, then click **Join as a business**. Complete the online form as prompted.

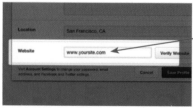

2 **Verify your website address**
When you verify your website address you will be allocated a little tick next to your website address on your Pinterest profile. If you do not have this tick on your profile then click the pencil to the right.

Enter your website address and then click Verify Website

Follow the instructions on the next page. You can verify with an HTML file or a META tag. If you are unsure about this then it may be worth speaking to your website developers and asking them to do this for you.

Verifying your Pinterest account allows you access to Analytics.

Verify Your Website

Why verify?   Verified sites show up on profile and in search results

How to verify   Download Verification File

                     Upload this file (pinterest-84bd7.html) to business.pinterest.com

Can't upload a file? Verify with a meta tag   Do This Later   Complete Verification

When your website is verified, then you will see the checkmark next to the website address. You will also be able to view the analytics from your site.

Your profile & Pins

Settings

Analytics

Make sure your Pinterest page is SEOd (search engine optimized) with full keyword-rich descriptions in every area.
Your Pinterest page can actually impact your website's SEO. Everything from the name of your account, to the alt text on your images can affect your search results.

3 **Edit your Business Account Settings**

In this area you can change your email notifications and link your other social networking platforms. It is also the area where you can deactivate your account if needed.

Click on your name at the top then scroll down to **Settings**

Pinterest   +   Julia Doherty · ...

                                                                 Your profile & Pins

Business account basics   **Settings**

                                                                 Analytics

Email address   **Find friends**

                                                                 Follow boards

Password   Change your password...   **Visit the Help Centre**

Language   **English (UK)**   Log out

Profile checklist

 Does your Pinterest name include a keyword about your business, as well as your business name?

Changing your name is relatively straightforward. Simply click the pencil to the right of your profile

Ensure this area is completed in full.

You have 200 characters in the **About you** section so use this space wisely. Make sure that you keep it engaging and not overly keyword-y.

Unlike LinkedIn and Facebook, your username on Pinterest can be changed as often as you wish. Your username forms the website address that will direct people to your Pinterest account. If it is a business account, then make sure that your website has been verified (see page 250).

The location is also important. If you are a local business then add the city or town as well as the country.

② Have you connected your social networking platforms?

From the settings page, scroll down and select the relevant social networking platforms.

Social Networks

f Not connected		
Log in with Facebook	No	Use your Facebook account to log in
🐦 Not connected		
Log in with Twitter	No	Use your Twitter account to log in
8+ Not connected to Google+		
Connect with Google+	No	Connect to Google+
M Not connected to Gmail		
Connect with Gmail	No	Connect to Gmail
🆈! Not connected to Yahoo		
Connect with Yahoo	No	Connect to Yahoo

As previously mentioned, you can connect your Facebook business page to Pinterest via a third party application called Pinvolve. **http://www.pinvolve.co/**

The Pinvolve Team has a Pinterest account, which you may be interested in following: **http://www.pinterest.com/pinvolve/**

This is their profile on the "Meet the team" board, which sums up the company:

Downloading the Facebook application called Pinvolve allows you to pin images to your Facebook business page.

The Pinvolve Team

We are a young start-up developing a kick-ass collage app for the iPad called Bazaart. Since most of our attention is currently being put into our product development, we felt the pain of having to maintain online marketing presence on Facebook and Pinterest. Instead of being frustrated, we decided to build Pinvolve. We are geeky smart like that. Pinvolve makes repinning, sharing and tweeting your Facebook, Pinterest, and Instagram content, directly from your Facebook fan page, easy as pie.

Source: http://www.pinterest.com/pinvolve/the-pinvolve-team/

Pinterest boards are where you collect Pins. For example, if you were refurbishing your office, then you may have a Pinterest board called "Office refurb ideas". When you see an image (or Pin) of a desk or a cupboard that would look great in your new office, then you would pin the image to your board. You then build your boards with your collection of images.

Board checklist

Do you have a minimum of five boards?

If you do not have a minimum of five boards, then your Pinterest account will appear inactive and very new. So this is your first goal. Choose topics or categories that reflect your business values, culture, interests, products and services. Be creative with your board names!

If you are a business owner then here are a few ideas of popular boards to get you started. Remember to pin as much from your website as possible.

● The blog
● Books worth reading
● Quotations
● Infographics
● Meet the team
● Guest bloggers
● Facebook pictures
● Our products
● Our services
● Portfolios
● Technology
● Things I like
● To create a board, click on the + button next to your name, and then scroll down to **Create a board**

You can add new boards from your profile or while you're Pinning, and you can always edit a board if you ever need to change its name or description.

⬆ Upload a Pin

🌐 Add from a website

▦ Create a board

The Pin It button is the easiest way to Pin things from around the web.

Make sure that each board has a full description, including some good keywords. Choose a category and then add a location if needed.

You will see the option for a **Secret** board. A secret board can be shared with other selected pinners and is not in the public domain. A secret board can be used for a number of reasons, such as organizing a surprise party, showcasing ideas for a new project that has not yet been launched, or even as a Christmas gift list. You can have unlimited secret boards.

Create a Board	×
Name*	e.g. For the Home
Description	Add a short description to your board
Category	Choose a category ▼
Add a map?	No
Secret	No Learn more
	Cancel Create Board

Does each board have a description?

If you have existing boards, then please go back and see if they have a full description. If you created your Pinterest boards a while ago, then it is worth checking all of your boards to make sure that they have a description.

Originally, Pinterest would not allow descriptions at the initial stage of creation. Therefore, there are many boards out there that do not have a full description. The description of your board is a key aspect to being found in the search results.

To add or change a description to a board that has already been created follow these instructions:

Click on **Your profile & Pins**.

Your profile & Pins
Settings
Analytics
Find friends
Follow boards

Hot tip

To maximize search results, make sure that you have added a description to your Pinterest boards.

...cont'd

Find the board that you wish to change, click **Edit**, then change or add the description by completing the field as shown below.

Edit board / Our Portfolio   ✕

Name	Our Portfolio
Description	This board represents our design portfolio. It may be Facebook cover photos, Twitter skins and headers, LinkedIn pages, youtube skins. We even put together forum signatures and complete fan pages. www.green-umbrella.biz

Do you have relatively short titles?

Boards with shorter titles are more likely to be followed. Active pinners are usually very visual people, and not necessarily big readers. Therefore, having short and to-the-point titles for your boards will give you an advantage over other pinners.

Do you have a minimum of five pins in each of your boards?

It is best not to launch a board unless you have a minimum of five pins. Not only does the board look a little unloved if it has one lonely pin sitting there, but it also gives the impression that you are not an active pinner.

Add a pin to a board

There are numerous ways in which you can add a pin to a board.

 Upload a pin from your computer

If you have an image that you would like to upload from a computer (a popular way of uploading photos), then follow these steps:

First click on the + and select Upload a Pin

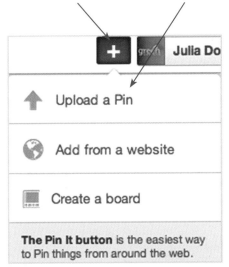

Select your image by clicking Choose image

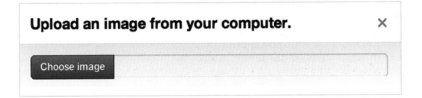

Select which board you would like to allocate the image to, add a description and choose if you would like to share this pin with your social networking platforms.

...cont'd

Select your board

Add a description

Share the pin

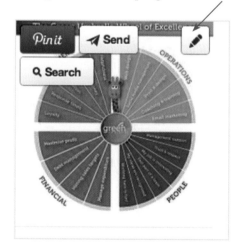

Once you click **Pin it** your image will appear in the newsfeed to be showcased to your network. To find the image again, simply click on your board.

If you would like to add a website link to an image that you have uploaded from your computer, then you will first need to click in your board and source the image. Simply hover over the image and click the pencil in the top right-hand corner.

Don't forget

There are two main ways to upload a Pin – from your computer and from a website.

From here you can add your source/website link. This is also the area where you can delete the pin if you no longer wish to have it showcased on your Pinterest account.

Edit Pin   ×

Board	Green Umbrella Stuff
Description	Do you measure how successful your business is? This is how Green Umbrella Social Media for Business does it.
Source	http://www.green-umbrella.biz/2014/01/measur

Delete Pin   Cancel   Save changes

2 **Upload a pin from a website**

There are two ways to pin from a website.

a) Click the + button and then click Add from a website

Enter the website address that you wish to pin from then click Next

...cont'd

You can then hover over any of the images displayed and click the **Pin it** button to pin that image to your relevant board.

When other pinners then click on the image, they will be sent to the original source (the website).

b) Using the Pin it button

This is the most popular way of pinning an image from a website.

Download the Pin it button for your web browser
(Find out more by visiting http://about.pinterest.com/goodies/)

You will then have a small Pinterest button on your web browser that looks similar to this (this is the Google Chrome version).

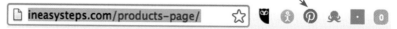

If you are visiting a website and you see an image that you would like to add to one of your Pinterest boards then just click your **Pin it** button on your web browser. Pinterest will then display all of the images available on the selected page of the website that you are able to upload to your Pinterest board. Once again, simply hover over the image and then pin your image to your selected board by clicking the **Pin it** button.

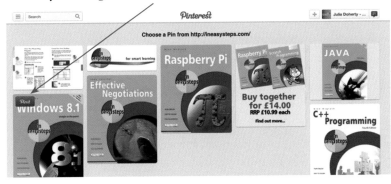

If you are a user of Google Chrome, then you will notice that most images on a website will display a **Pin it** button when you hover over the image. This can prove irritating for people who are not Pinterest advocates, and you can turn it off if you feel the need. Simply right click on the installed **Pin it** button.

Then place a tick in the Hide Button box to hide hovering Pin it buttons

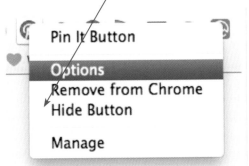

Now you know how to pin to your boards, then double check each board to see if they have a minimum of five pins in each.

If you are using Google Chrome as your preferred browser, then you will see a Pin it button on every image when you hover your mouse over the image.

Individual pin checklist

Pinterest is introducing new pin variations all the time, so it is worth subscribing to the Pinterest blog to make sure that you are keeping up with new opportunities. Visit **http://blog.pinterest.com/**

Here are the basic checks for your individual pins:

1 **Does each pin have a description?**

It is imperative to check that your pins have a description as this is picked up on the Pinterest search and also by other search engines.

2 **Check the source of your pin**

Pinterest is in the public domain and, therefore, copyright rules still apply. Check the small print for Pinterest copyright by visiting **http://about.pinterest.com/copyright/**

Checking the source of your pin is extremely important. Always check the source of your pin if you are re-pinning others' content. If you click on the pin and the landing page is a false URL, or an error site, then do not re-pin it. You can also report it or leave a comment on the pin to warn others. Sometimes, pinners will use a popular image, but then the source of the pin will lead to their own website rather than the site of the original source. This is unethical pinning and, therefore, do not re-pin and only give credit where credit is due.

3 **Have you added a watermark?**

If you are creating your own images then consider adding a stamp or watermark. This way, the content will always stay connected to your brand and will continue to promote you whenever the post is re-pinned. It is also a deterrent for others who wish to use your image, but not give you the credit for it.

If you are not a designer, but you still wish to add a watermark to your pins, then have a look at a free and easy to use tool called PicMonkey: **http://www.picmonkey.com/**

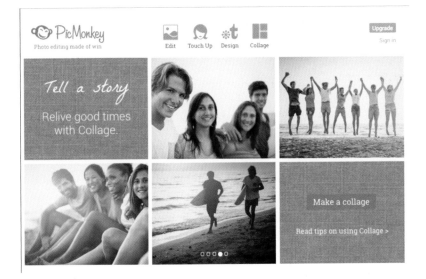

 Take advantage of rich pins

Pinterest offers rich pins for products, articles, recipes and movies to any brand. If you add a rich pin, then you have the opportunity to pin much more information on the pin than regular pins. It is not a simple process to add rich pins to your account. To find out how, visit **https://developers.pinterest.com/rich_pins/**

 Are your pins optimized for Twitter?

You may not be Tweeting your pins, but others may! Try to keep your descriptions under 140 characters and utilize hashtags within your descriptions. Make it easy for others to share your content with their audience.

6 **Are you utilizing other software to make your images wonderful?**

There are numerous tools that have been built to support Pinterest and the majority of these are free to the end user. As well as PicMonkey, which is a free and easy to use online software, the following tools are also worthy of a mention.

The first tool is called Pinstamatic. Visit **www.pinstamatic.com**

...cont'd

This tool can be used to create a whole range of images:

- Pin a website
- Pin a quote
- Pin a sticky note
- Pin from Spotify
- Pin from a Twitter account
- Pin a date
- Pin a place
- Edit one of your own images

You can save the images and use them on your other social networking sites, or pin them straight from Pinstamatic to your Pinterest account.

Another popular tool for pinning websites to your Pinterest account is called Snapito (**visit http://snapito.com/**)

Also consider looking at Instagram (**http://instagram.com/**), Pixlr (**http://pixlr.com/**) and Tweegram (**http://www.tweegram. com/**).

 Are you posting a mix of pictures and videos?

Images are not the only things that you can pin on Pinterest – you can pin videos too!

Pinning direct from YouTube or from your website is often an oversight. However, videos are extremely powerful. If you have an active YouTube/Vimeo account or you create videos for your business, then ensure that you are pinning them to your Pinterest account.

Either click the Pinterest icon in the social sharing toolbar, as shown below:

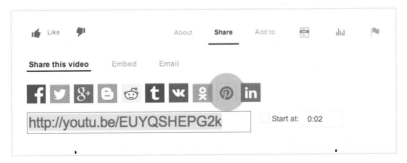

Or use the Google Chrome **Pin it** button when you hover over the video.

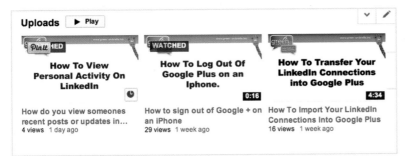

Implement a content strategy

Pinterest is no different to any other marketing and you need to plan your content, engagement and listening strategy to be an effective marketer on this platform. Here are some strategies to consider:

Research

Have a look at others within your industry to see what they are pinning, but also have a look at your target market to see what type of images are of interest to them and what boards have they set up. Look at your emails. Are you often answering questions to solve people's problems? If so, then consider adding a board where you can showcase these answers.

Searching on Pinterest is easy.

 Enter your search term

 Select from pins, boards or pinners

≡	welly rack			*Pinterest*	+	Julia Doherty ...
Pins	Boards	Pinners				Search results for "welly rack"

Remember your boards

It can be too easy to forget some boards that you have created, as you will find yourself pinning to certain boards on a more regular basis. Make a conscious effort to pin across a range of boards as this will stretch your imagination and keep your boards alive.

Remember to follow other pinners

Search and follow other users or individual boards that are of interest to you.

From the search box at the top of your Pinterest account, you can find results for pins (default), boards or pinners. This is the main reason why you should be adding descriptions to your pins, boards and profiles.

≡	pinterest tips	🔍
Pins	**Boards**	**Pinners**

Hot tip

You need to let people know that you exist, and following others is a good way to start. You will be amazed how many people will follow you back as soon as you start repinning their content. It is also a good source for content for your own boards.

Remember to add website addresses to your descriptions
The more information about the source of a pin the better it is for website traffic and general brand awareness.

Check ALL your pins
Whether you are re-pinning or you are creating your own pins, always double check the pin to make sure that the link works.

Do not pin-overload!
It is tempting to spend time on Pinterest and then pin many images in one go, but refrain from doing this as you will flood your newsfeed and your audience will not be happy.

Time your pins
When are your followers online the most? The easiest way to find out is to take a look at a company called Tailwind: **http://www.tailwindapp.com/**

If you can post your blog or new products at the times that your network is online the most, then how powerful will that be for your business?

Produce pinnable content
80% of all Pins are re-pins, so make sure that your own content has the "re-pin factor".

Add fabulous images to your blog
If you start investing in images for each blog article, you are likely to see a dramatic increase in the traffic from Pinterest to your website.

Have a play with different sizes
Tall pins are more noticeable in the newsfeed, but try not to make them too long. Your pin can be 554 pixels wide without restriction on length, and up to 5,000 pixels high. Some infographics work well as a long pin.

Hot tip

As part of your Pinterest strategy, consider using some Pinterest scheduling tools such as the ViralTag application within Hootsuite, or Viralwoot (https://viralwoot.com/)

Hot tip

You could use Dreamstime (http://www.dreamstime.com/), as some of the free images are excellent and the paid for images are very good and not that expensive. Other popular stock images can be sourced from http://www.istockphoto.com/ http://www.shutterstock.com/ or www.dollarphotoclub.com (to name a few).

Conclusion

1 Build your platform

Have you created a business Pinterest account, which has been edited correctly? Do you have at least five boards, which all have a minimum of five pins within them? Have you chosen a cover photo for each of those boards? Have you verified your website and received the checkmark on your account? Have you pinned the key features of your business to your Pinterest account from your website? Have you added the **Pin it** button to your website and social sharing tools? If you can say "yes" to the majority of the above, then congratulations, you have reached stage one of Pinterest success.

2 Grow your network

Have you emailed your database to let them know about your Pinterest account? Have you added a link to your email signature? Have you added a Pinterest icon with a link on your website? Have you followed people within your target market? Have you also commented and re-pinned others' content to engage with your audience? Do you have a strategy to cross-promote your pins on Facebook, Twitter, Google+ and other social networking platforms? Do you embed your Pinterest boards into your blog articles? Utilizing collaborative boards will help with growing your network on Pinterest.

Pinterest can be a slow burn to get your number of followers increased significantly. Therefore, do not expect thousands of followers immediately. It takes time to build, but the investment is worth it.

If you are investing time in the above strategies to grow your network, then congratulations, you have reached stage two of Pinterest success.

3 Implement a strategy

Once you have your initial boards created then it is time to consider your strategy for pinning and engagement.

Have you done your research? Do you have a strategy to check those forgotten boards? Do you have a strategy to follow other pinners? Do you check all pins for correct links? Are you pinning consistently? Do you know the best time of the day to pin those important sales pins? Are you utilizing design tools to give your pins the "re-pin factor"? Are you adding fabulous images to your blog? Have you experimented with different size images to see what works best on your account? Are you promoting your pins through contents? Have you joined any community boards?

If you have a defined written strategy, which is being implemented for Pinterest then congratulations, you have now reached stage three of Pinterest success.

 ### Measure the results

In August 2014 Pinterest introduced the new and very powerful analytics tool. This is completely free of charge and will enlighten you with many analytics, such as metrics about the people who engage with your business and other topics that they are interested in. You can also view your audience's most common interests at a glance and you can tailor your marketing strategy around this information.

If you are a numbers person then you will probably enjoy the statistics on number of impressions, repins and clicks.

The analytics tool is only available to those that have registered a business account. Simply go to **https://analytics.pinterest.com/** to find out your statistics.

If you are measuring your results, tweaking your strategy to improve those results, then congratulations, you have reached stage four of Pinterest success.

Remember, it is OK if your Pinterest account does not have a million followers, because it takes time to build something amazing. Just keep engaging with your users, putting out great content and being a good member of the Pinterest community, and your hard work will be rewarded.

Checklist

Have a look at the checklist below and see how you have scored.

 1   Have you set up a business account? ☐

 2   Have you verified your website? ☐

 3   Does your Pinterest name include a keyword about your business, as well as your business name? ☐

 4   Do you have a minimum of five Pinterest boards? ☐

 5   Does each board have a full description? ☐

 6   Do you have relatively short titles for your boards? ☐

 7   Do you have a minimum of five pins in each of your boards? ☐

 8   Does each individual pin have a full description? ☐

 9   Do your pins contain a content source? i.e. Does it link to a website? ☐

 10   Are you posting a mix of images and videos? ☐

8 Google Plus

An introduction to Google Plus

Google Plus is another social networking site that was launched in 2011. Google is keen to dominate the online world and Google Plus is its way of taking on the big boys such as Twitter and Facebook.

Like many others, I was one of those people who signed up to Google Plus (or more commonly known as G+ or Google+) in the early days, when it was "invitation only". With the exception of automating my blogs into Google Plus, I was very rarely active on this platform. I was under the impression that no one talked on Google Plus, even though I had lots of connections in my circles. I think I had good reasons to be apprehensive about Google Plus as I was a victim of Google's previous attempts at building a social networking site:

- **Google Wave**, which was launched in 2009. Everyone was excited and could not wait to get our invitations to join this amazing social networking platform. Then Google shut it down a year later.
- **Google Buzz** was yet another attempt at creating a social networking site that was launched in 2010. Again, I spent time developing my platform, building my audience etc., only to find that less than 12 months later, Google pulled the plug!

So when they announced Google Plus in October 2011, like many others, I was understandably apprehensive about spending any time on this new platform.

We are now in 2015 and Google Plus is still going strong, so perhaps we should embrace this social networking site, as it appears to be standing the test of time and more and more people are talking about it. Since actively using this platform, I have seen some astounding results; consider spending some time here, especially if "driving traffic to your website" was one of your main goals that you set in Chapter 1.

Reasons to be active on Google Plus

Integration with other Google Products

How clever is Google? If you are a business owner then you will be using some of Google's products already, from general searching of the Internet, to Gmail, Google Docs, YouTube, Google places and a whole range of other products. Google Plus is the glue that holds all these products together, and it is constructed in a genius way. You will probably have a Google Plus account and not even realize it.

Google Circles

Google Circles are a more natural way to manage your friendships. They encourage you to talk only to a specific target market, therefore enabling you to keep the conversation real and relevant without flooding your timeline with white noise. Google Circles are discussed in more detail later in this chapter.

The mobile apps are fabulous

The Google Plus mobile apps on both Android and iOS load much faster than their competitors'. The Google Plus app is also a better design and it is a pleasure to work with. The images are clear, and the general look and feel of the app is encouraging to use.

Control

Google has a feature called "Data Liberation", which means you can pack up all your data, from files, photos, spreadsheets, etc. and walk away with it at anytime, easily. It is all stored under one roof.

Photos

If you are using the iPhone app then Google Plus will automatically store your photos from your iPhone into Google Plus, enabling you to click a share button and share those images with your network if you so wish. Alternatively, you can just keep them private for your eyes only. The tagging feature within Google Plus is also impressive. It offers better privacy features and it is good to see that they do not have the facial recognition as a default.

Hangouts

Hangouts is certainly one of the best features of Google Plus. Hangouts is like chat rooms or online meetings and is free to use. Hangouts are great, since they can be integrated with YouTube.

...cont'd

Easier profile setup

Setting up your Google Plus profile is a breeze compared to Facebook. If you are already using some of Google's other products then some of the hard work will already be completed for you. Profile checklist is covered later in this chapter.

Browser Integration

Google has something that Facebook, Twitter, LinkedIn or Pinterest do not have and that is its own browser, Google Chrome. With added Chrome extensions, you can make your life so much easier.

Better Search

Google is the number one search engine in the world, and it is learning all the time. Having a Google Plus account enables Google to return search results that are relevant to you specifically. Search is the foundation of Google and no one can argue that they know their stuff.

Notification system

Notifications are great. Even if you are not an active Google Plus user, you will be drawn into Google Plus by the notifications you will see on the top right of your Google Search page. Like many of us, we naturally want to clear the notifications so that there are no red numbers outstanding. The notification system that Google presents also allows you to do several things from within the notification pop-up system (even if you are not actually in Google Plus at the time. How cool is that?).

No friend requests

Google Plus is a little bit more like Twitter, as you simply follow people on Google Plus and add them to your circles (lists). There is no "will you be my friend" scenario on Google Plus.

Better game implementation

On Facebook, you may find game notifications from sites such as Farmville, or Words With Friends a little annoying. Even though you can block these requests on Facebook, it is still a pain and may flood your notification area. This does not happen on Google Plus at the moment.

Safer sharing

Google Plus lets you assign a privacy level to each and every piece of content that you post with your network. This is discussed in more detail later in the chapter, but this is an extremely powerful feature of Google Plus.

Fabulous for business

Google Plus makes it easy to create a page and presence for your business. Others can give you reviews, add photos and appear in Google searches. Having a presence for your business on Google Plus is a total no-brainer as it helps with both visibility and Google ranking.

Complete and optimize your profile

As with any social networking site, it is important to have a completed profile, and Google Plus is no exception. If ranking highly in Google is important to you, then it is probably more important to have a completed profile on Google Plus than any other platform. So let's talk through the steps to get you started.

First of all, you need to set up a personal profile.

 Visit **https://plus.google.com/** then click **Create an Account**

2 Complete all the fields to set up your account and click on **Next Step** to complete the setup process

To complete your personal profile:

1 On the far left click **Home**, then scroll down and click **Profile**

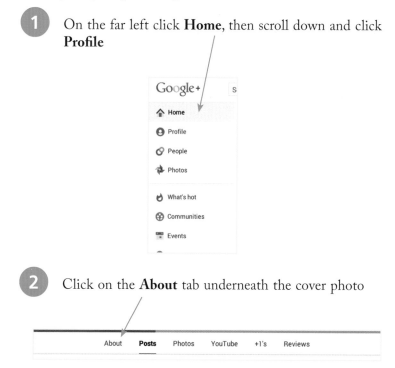

2 Click on the **About** tab underneath the cover photo

We are now going to work through the various sections with tips on each.

At the bottom of each area you will see an **Edit** tab. Click here to edit each section. It is worth taking your time to build this area.

Tagline – this should ideally include a target keyword as it is highly indexed by Google.

Story

Tagline
Social media junkie, gadget geek and an outdoors girl!

...cont'd

Introduction – there is no right or wrong way to put together your introduction. However, it is best to keep it brief with keyword rich text, and use hyperlinks within the text to drive traffic back to your website. It is also important to make it easy for people to contact you.

To hyperlink a word (make it turn blue so that visitors to your profile can click on the blue word and be sent to your website) is easy.

Simply highlight the word with your mouse that you wish to into a link, then click **Link**

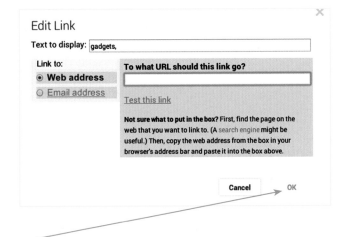

Decide if you would like to direct people to an email address or a website and enter the relevant destination details in the appropriate area.

Click **OK** to save the settings

Add a **Contact me** area with a hyperlink to an email address at the bottom of this section

Complete all other areas in full, including links to your other social networking platforms, your blog and websites, your education and your contact information. Resist progressing further with Google Plus until this area is completed.

3 Look at your avatar (or personal profile image) and the cover photo

The golden rule is to make sure that you are adding an image of *you* on your personal profile, not a logo of your company. The logo should be added to your business page (see page 239). Your profile image will appear in numerous places. Therefore, it is important to have a good head and shoulder image of yourself so that you are easily recognized.

To add a profile picture, simply hover over the area and then click on the camera icon

...cont'd

- Upload a new photo; choose one from your albums or take a new picture
- Crop and edit your photo
- Click **Set as profile photo** when you've finished

Any new profile photo that you upload from your computer will also be saved in your public **Profile photos** album and can be accessed from **Albums**.

Adding your cover photo

Your cover photo can help to make a great first impression when others visit your profile. So, if you can, ask a designer to put a nice image together for you, or to choose an image that represents you and your business. You never get a second chance to make a first impression, and your cover photo says a lot about you and your business.

To add your new cover photo, simply hover over the current cover photo area and then click on the **Change cover** link

You can then choose from a template that Google offers you, or you can upload your own, or select from your photos and albums.

Use the cropping tools to get the best image possible and then click **Select Cover Photo** when you have finished.

- Recommended size: 1080 x 608 pixels
- Minimum size: 480 x 270 pixels
- Maximum size: 2120 x 1192 pixels

4 Control your sharing settings

Google Plus enables you to manage who can interact with you and your posts, who can tag you in photos, when you would like to receive notifications, and lots more. So now it is time to edit these settings to ensure that your Google Plus experience is a pleasant one.

Navigate back to the menu on the right hand side and then click **Settings** towards the bottom of the list.

Work your way through the settings. This may take some time, but it is time well invested, as your Google Plus experience will be affected by the results of these settings.

Have you included five photos for your profile?
Your Google Plus personal photos are found on the main tab.

- The tabs are revealed for your personal photos.
- You can add up to five photos that are viewable to the public on your profile. Change your images on a regular basis. The gurus say every two weeks, although this may not always be practical.

If you are trying to add images to this area of your profile, there are two main factors that allocate an image to **Photos of you** and display it on your profile so it is viewable by the public.

- The image MUST be tagged with your name
- The image MUST be shared publicly

Failure to tick both these boxes will mean that the image will not appear in the **Photos of you** section on your profile.

...cont'd

To add photos to the **Photos of you** area:

 Click on **Home** then click **Photos**

 Select **Upload photos** then choose your image from your computer

 Click the face or an area on the image to enable you to tag yourself

4 Start typing your name and then select your name from the dropdown menu below. Select your name to tag yourself in the image

 Share your image in the public domain. Once this is completed, your image will appear in the **Photos of you** section

Create a business page

Once you have established your personal profile on Google Plus, it is time to set up your business page.

1 Log in to Google Plus

2 Click on **Home** then scroll down to **Pages**

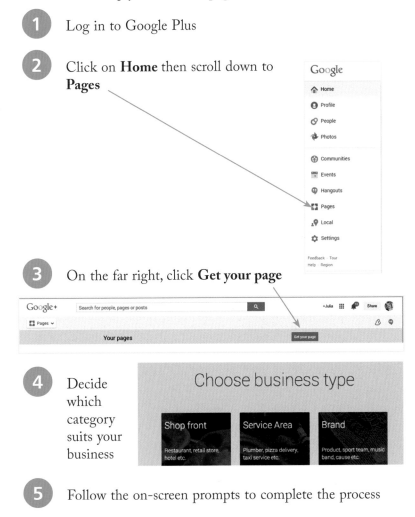

3 On the far right, click **Get your page**

4 Decide which category suits your business

Choose business type

Shop front — Restaurant, retail store, hotel etc.

Service Area — Plumber, pizza delivery, taxi service etc.

Brand — Product, sport team, music band, cause etc.

5 Follow the on-screen prompts to complete the process

6 Once your page is completed, then your business will appear in Google Local Search (on all devices).

Your Google+ content in Search: your page, along with your most recent posts, is eligible to show on the right-hand side of Google search results

Hot tip

The more content you post, the stronger your presence can be on Google.

Grow your circles

Any type of social networking activity is to "grow your network". Without growing your network, you are really just talking to yourself.

With Google Plus you achieve this by adding people to your circles. Circles are a simple way to categorize people into lists. In a similar way to putting people into lists on Twitter, or adding interest lists on Facebook, in Google Plus you add people to circles.

Then what do you do with them?

You should think about your circles in three different ways:

Inbound Circles – these are people you may be interested in following but will not want to market to. For example, you could set up inbound circles for:

- Friends and family
- Interesting gurus
- Clients and customers
- Competitors

Outbound Circles – these are lists of people you can potentially want to market to. For example, if you're in the recruitment business you could have a circle of recruiters and those who are involved in the recruitment industry. If you produce a blog article and then post it on your Google Plus account, you can send this to the newsfeed of all those in your Recruitment Circles. This is extremely powerful, as you can also tick a box that says "Also email to this circle", so the recipients will receive a message in their inbox. Currently, no other social networking platform will allow you to do this.

Extended Circles – you will also have the option to send your post to "Extended circles". This simply means sending your post not only to the people in your circles, but also to the people in their circles.

There is an art in posting on Google Plus, but this is covered later in the chapter. Let's first build your network and explain how to find people to connect with.

How to connect with new people:

1 Click **Home**, then **People**

2 Use **Suggestions** to find people who have already added you to circles. You may be surprised to see some of the names in this area, but Google knows who you are connected to elsewhere on the Internet, so it is very clever with its suggestions on who to connect with

Once you have created your circles then it is time to start producing that all-important content.

Share your content with others

What type of posts should you be sharing?
If you produce a text-only post, then you are likely to get little or no interaction with your audience (unless you are asking a particular question). If, however, you attach an image, audio clip or video then you are much more likely to have engagement on the post. So, try to incorporate some type of visual with every single post that you place on Google Plus.

With regard to content of the posts, well, that is completely up to you. Each business is different and we all have different target markets. The best tips are:

- **Be genuine.** Only post content that you would enjoy reading or viewing yourself. Think of your audience, what would they be interested in? What would they like to see? If you have your network at the forefront of your mind each time you construct a new post then you will be onto a winner.

- **Be creative.** Don't just post a "quote of the day"; add your comments as to what that quote means to you. Don't just post a picture of something beautiful; explain why you are posting it. Don't just post the link to your blog; give a teaser to your network as to what people will find out when they read the full article. Putting that little bit of effort into your posts on Google Plus will create interest in you and your brand.

There are many "gurus" out there in the Google Plus world, but there is one particular person who stands out from the crowd. His name is Guy Kawasaki and he is a real guru when it comes to Google Plus. Take a look at the types of posts that he produces by visiting his profile here: **https://plus.google.com/u/0/+GuyKawasaki/posts**

You will notice that every single post has an image attached to it. There are posts about his personal life as well as his business life. There are numerous posts that he simply finds interesting and wants to share with his audience. He is completely genuine and this shines through on Google Plus.

...cont'd

How often should you share posts on Google Plus?
Now there is the ultimate question! When I first started I was posting about 15 times a day until one person messaged me to say that I was flooding his newsfeed. I have found my sweet spot to be between 4-6 posts a day, spread from 6am to 9pm. Having some consistency in the types of posts that you produce certainly helps.

Here is a typical day for me on Google Plus, with regard to content that I produce:

Post 1 (6am) – I usually post, "What's on your agenda today?". I then post a few things that I have on my list, which will encompass some personal bits as well. I attach a picture of a quote, or something inspirational to go with this post to get people inspired about their forthcoming day.

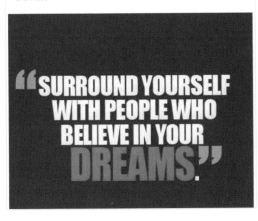

...cont'd

Post 2 – I am usually "checking in" somewhere. Whether that be the office, a client's premises, or the venue where I may be speaking at some event. Using the location icon on Google Plus, I attach a photo of where I am or what I am doing.

Post 3 – I will share an article that appears in my RSS feeds from software that I am registered with called "Savvy". I receive a daily email from Savvy with relevant articles on my topic of expertise. I rarely share these articles on any of my other social networking sites, so the content that I produce on Google Plus is unique and not just regurgitated content from my other social networking platforms.

Post 4 – Is usually an article from my website, a link to my podcast, or a YouTube video that we have produced. (Part of my 20% content).

Post 5 (9pm-ish) – a closing post for the evening. I have got into the habit of posting a beautiful picture along with my closing thoughts for the day.

You can post what you like, and how often you like, but I recommend getting into a habit of consistency and then you will reap the rewards. I am now receiving regular comments from others to tell me what their plans are for the day, which is brilliant. And the interaction I am receiving on my "goodnight" posts is also excellent.

If you have a chance to promote others' content then please do so. Remember to "tag" them in the post by typing + in front of their name.

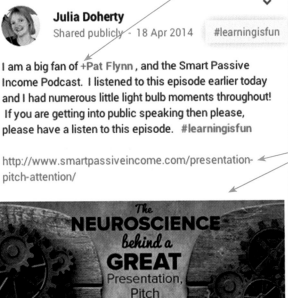

Add an image, then post the link in the content of the update for better engagement

Schedule your posts

Google Plus is not a platform that allows you to schedule posts from a social media management tool such as Hootsuite or TweetDeck. Even today, you can schedule posts into your Google Plus business page using Hootsuite but you cannot schedule a post to your Google Plus personal profile.

Google Plus has its pros and cons.

Pros

It is great that we do not have lots of noise on Google Plus, like we do on Twitter, Facebook and even LinkedIn, as you actually have to be present on the platform to post.

Cons

It is very difficult to plan your content and have consistency in your posts throughout the day if you are a busy person, or you do not wish to outsource your content creation.

However, there is a tool called **Do Share** that can help with this. Do Share is a Google Chrome extension that allows you to schedule messages into your Google Plus personal account. It is not the best software, but it does work if used correctly.

The key thing you must remember with Do Share is that you need to have Google Chrome open when the post is due to be sent to the network. If you have closed your computer, then it will not send (unlike Hootsuite or other social media management tools).

Google will more than likely release the API (application programming interface) for scheduling at some time in the future, but, at the time of going to print, this is the only software that allows you to schedule posts.

Get reviews on your business page

There are a number of ways to use reviews as part of your strategy to increase brand awareness for your business.

Give and you shall receive

If you are a local business then it is important to make sure that other businesses in the area know all about your business, and using the review function is a fabulous way to do this. Here's an example:

Let's say that I am running a local hairdressing salon. I need to think to myself, "Where is my key target market going to hangout? What will they be Googling to find telephone numbers and website addresses of other local places?" People who care about their appearance may also be interested in:

- The local gym
- The local leisure center
- The local spa
- Yoga club
- Tanning salon
- Local schools
- Hotels in the area
- Golf or tennis clubs

So, if my local hairdressing salon is leaving testimonials or reviews for all of the above places, then the chance that my target market will see my business online has been heightened by this activity.

Ask and you shall receive

As a marketer you will understand the importance of receiving testimonials for your business, and Google Plus is a fabulous way to collect them. Get into the habit of requesting testimonials or reviews on Google Plus as soon as you have completed a piece of work for a client or customer. If you are in the retail sector, then make sure you have a poster on your counter or shop window to say "Find us on Google Plus, and give us a review".

For example, I give out the address: "**www.green-umbrella. biz/review**" but if you put this into any web browser you are automatically directed to my Google Plus review page. (Pretty Link enables me to add a redirect for any target URL).

The more local business reviews you can get then the more brand awareness you will have online.

If you have a WordPress website, then consider the plugin called "Pretty Link". This free plugin allows you to manage any URL with an easy-to-remember URL.

Leave a review for another business

1   Click on the top right icon (your avatar)

2   Switch to your business page

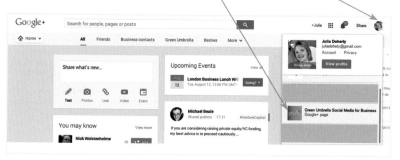

3   You will see that the avatar now represents your business page rather than your personal page

4   Search for the company that you wish to review

5   Select the company from the dropdown menu

6   Click the small pencil to write your review

Use this process to get your company name and brand to the market place.

Recommend other businesses

If you are a local business then it is important to make sure that your business is following other businesses in the local area.

 Log in to Google Plus and click on your avatar in the far right hand corner

 Switch to your company name from the dropdown menu

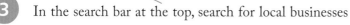

In the search bar at the top, search for local businesses

Select the place from the dropdown menu

Click on the pencil to write your review

Give the company a star rating

Write a short positive review for the business

Click publish to submit your review

If you write numerous reviews and tips about local businesses, then these reviews will be seen by lots of people in the local area. e.g. If you write a review on your local estate agent's page, then anyone who is searching for a house will also see that review. If they also see your reviews on local restaurants, etc., you will quickly be known as someone who knows the local area very well. This is a fabulous brand awareness strategy.

Verify your business

In September 2013 Google shut down the verification process for business pages. This was a fabulous function as you received a little check mark on your page.

Although the verification request process has been withdrawn for pages, you can still verify your account if you have a local places page. If you have set your page up as a local page, with a zip code or postcode, allocated a pin in the map, and added your opening hours etc., then you can still verify the account. You can verify your account from the main dashboard area. You then have two options, to verify your account by phone or by postcard.

Verify by postcard

 On the postcard request screen, make sure your address is displayed correctly on your postcard.

Verification by postcard

There is also an option to add a contact name. Then simply click **Send postcard**.

2 You will receive a physical postcard in the mail which will have a verification PIN number printed on the card. Enter your PIN number from your dashboard to verify your business.

To verify your account via the telephone

1 Make sure you can directly answer your business phone number to receive your verification PIN.

 Verification by phone

2 Click **Verify by phone** to have a PIN number sent to your phone. This is an automated message.

3 Enter the PIN number from the message to verify your business.

Beware

You will not be able to update the business name on the account until the verification process is complete.

Google My Business

In June 2014, Google launched a new product called Google My Business. In simple terms, this is a one stop shop for all business owners. You can access your My Business area from within your Google Plus account. For more detailed instructions about the feature known as Google My Business please visit **https://www.google.com/business/**

As soon as you log in, you will be guided through a tour which is quite self-explanatory.

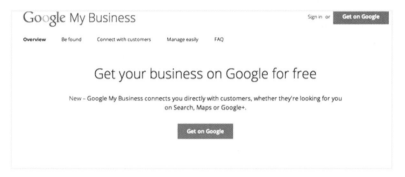

Once you are registered with My Business you will now be able to access the following, all from one screen:

- **Google+.** You can share new text, photos, links, videos, and events
- **Insights.** Once you verify your business you are able to gain insights into your visibility, engagement, and audience
- **Reviews.** Each business is given a Google rating and you are able to manage your reviews on Google and view other reviews around the web
- **Google Analytics.** Quick access directly to your Google Analytics dashboard
- **Start a Hangout.** With the click of a button you can start or join a Hangout

Connect to your YouTube channel

You can only link your YouTube channel to either your personal profile OR your business page. You are unable to link the channel to more than one profile. So you will need to decide which one you would prefer to have your channel linked to. Once you have your YouTube channel linked to a profile, each time you post a new video you could use RSS technology (see page 70) to automatically post to your Google Plus business page.

Once it is connected, you will be able to display your channel on the tab.

If you have not yet connected your YouTube account, then you can start this process by first visiting the advanced account settings: **https://www.youtube.com/account_advanced**

 Click **Connect with a Google+ page**

2 Choose a name. If you are linking your Google Plus page to your YouTube Channel, then you will not have a choice in your YouTube name. The channel will be named the same as your Google Plus page

There is no public link between your YouTube Channel and your Google Plus page/ profile unless you have publically linked them.

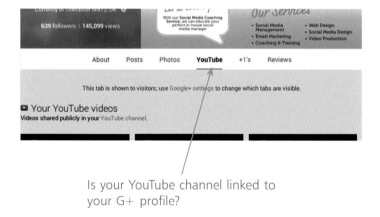

Is your YouTube channel linked to your G+ profile?

YouTube Analytics

YouTube also gives you useful information on your YouTube videos:

 Choose one of your videos and click **Analytics**

 YouTube will display analytics for your video

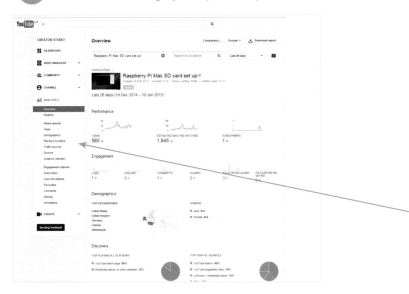

Hot tip

This is the just a summary of the popularity of your YouTube channel. Click on Demographics, Traffic sources, Devices or any of the other options on the left to drill down for further data.

Conclusion

 Build your platform

Have you built your business profile and page correctly? Have you added a cover photo and does your avatar display correctly? Have you verified your account, and added your social networking platforms to your account? Have you completed the "About us" area in as much detail as possible, including your full website address? If so, then congratulations, you have reached stage one of Google Plus success.

 Grow your network

Have you set up your circles for Google Plus? Have you connected to your other social networks such as Facebook and Twitter? Have you exported your LinkedIn connections and imported these into Google Plus? Perhaps you have a CRM system from which you can export the email addresses and add to Google Plus?

If you can confidently say that you are doing everything in your power to grow your network on Google Plus, then congratulations, you have reached stage two of Google Plus success for the small business owner.

3 **Implement a strategy**

Are you publishing content on a regular basis into Google Plus? A mix of content to include videos and photos? Are you also posting messages about your own business and educating your network about the services that you provide? Have you registered with **www.savvy.com** to receive relevant industry news that you can share on Google Plus? Have you downloaded the "Do Share" Google Chrome extension so that you can schedule your messages throughout the day? If you are a local business, do you have a strategy to give local tips on other businesses in the area?

If you feel that you are organized, and you have set your goals and objectives for Google Plus, and you have considered the majority of the above questions, then congratulations, you are en route to a successful Google Plus account.

(4) Measure the results

As with all marketing, it is important to measure your results, otherwise how do you know if you are being successful? Google is a little bit more complicated than the other sites as it incorporates so many other products, such as Google Analytics for your website, YouTube statistics, etc. Look at the basic statistics to make sure that your account is heading in the right direction. Take a note of:

- Followers of the account
- Number of views
- Also keep an eye on comments, likes and shares of public posts

There is a very cool feature within Google Plus called "Ripples". A Ripple can only be viewed on public posts, but they give some very insightful information.

To view a Ripple, and receive lots of information about a particular post, click the dropdown arrow in the top right hand corner of the post. Then click **View Ripples**

You can then view who has shared the content. From here you have an option to follow and engage with those individuals. This is quite a powerful tool if you have a competitor who is popular on Google Plus. You can see who is interacting with their posts and start following and engaging with that particular network

Checklist

Now it is your turn. Look through the list below and see how many ticks you can place in the boxes on the right.

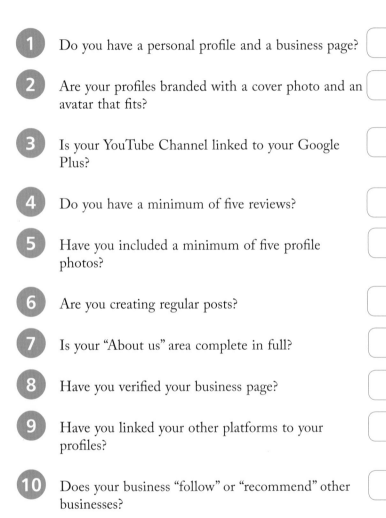

1 Do you have a personal profile and a business page?

2 Are your profiles branded with a cover photo and an avatar that fits?

3 Is your YouTube Channel linked to your Google Plus?

4 Do you have a minimum of five reviews?

5 Have you included a minimum of five profile photos?

6 Are you creating regular posts?

7 Is your "About us" area complete in full?

8 Have you verified your business page?

9 Have you linked your other platforms to your profiles?

10 Does your business "follow" or "recommend" other businesses?

9 Google Analytics

The final piece of the puzzle

Google Analytics (**www.google.com/analytics**) is an amazing, free tool that **all** website owners and anyone with online presence should take advantage of – it is a great opportunity. It tells you all the key information you'll need: How active is your website? Where is the traffic from your website coming from? Are your Facebook page and LinkIn page notifications working to create interest in your products? Do you need to change the topics for your blog? What are your most popular web pages? And, finally, is your website getting referrals from other sites?

There are many different metrics that you can measure within Google Analytics, but the main objective is to break it down into the core analytics that all business owners need to know.

1 **Add the code**

Once you have created your Google account, speak to your web designer who will add the tracking code (script) to the relevant areas of your website, and set you up with an account and analytics reports.

2 **What can you measure?**

When you first log in to Google Analytics it can be rather daunting. Here are the top three aspects that all business owners should measure:

Visitors
Figuring out how your website is being used, and using information to enhance your site ultimately starts with the visitor. Knowing who is coming to visit your site, how long they then spend on the site, and what pages they are looking at before leaving, can give you valuable insight into improving the functionality of your site.

Four metrics to look at on this overview report on a regular basis are:

● **Sessions**
● **Average Session Duration**
● **Bounce Rate**
● **New Visitors**

Sessions

This signifies the visitors that have spent any time on your website. The reason you should pay more attention to this statistic, rather than page views, is because you want to know that people are exploring your site, and that they are not "bots" or spam accounts.

Average Session Duration

You need to know that people are exploring your site and spending some quality time reading content. If your average session is under 30 seconds, then you know you need to add more relevant and engaging content to your site.

Bounce Rate

Bounce rate is the measurement of people who stay on your website for a short amount of time. It is rumored that the level set for Google Analytics bounce rate is 30 seconds. However, Google have never announced this. If you have a high bounce rate of 80%, it means that people have visited your website for 30 seconds or less and then navigated to another website.

Many people ask "What should my bounce rate be?". There isn't a right answer to that question, as every industry and audience is different. Sometimes a high bounce rate is not a bad thing. For example, if you want people to instantly sign up for your newsletter or download an eBook on that first initial page visit, then your bounce rate will be high, but you have converted a number of visitors.

New Visitors

It is important to ensure that your audience is growing consistently and that new people are visiting your website. Having a fine balance between returning visitors and brand new visitors is

...cont'd

important. Ultimately, you should watch your visitor metrics for major dips and peaks.

Acquisition

This is Google's language for "traffic sources". It is important to know where your traffic is coming from. Click **Acquisition** on the left hand column on Google Analytics' Overview page.

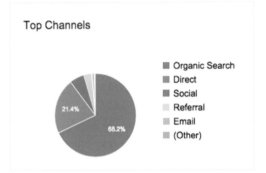

Top Channels

- Organic Search
- Direct
- Social
- Referral
- Email
- (Other)

21.4%

68.2%

Having a healthy balance of search, referral and direct traffic is good for your business.

If you have over 80% organic search or paid search traffic, and Google makes an algorithm change, you can lose money extremely quickly.

If you explore further into your Traffic Source report you can see which sources sent the most traffic. The "social" report is always intriguing, but you may also be interested to explore the other areas.

If you look at the individual source reports, you can see All Traffic, Direct, Referrals, Search and Campaigns. Campaigns is where your Pay Per Click accounts should live (see this in "how to" in Google Analytics Help: **https://support.google.com/analytics/?hl=en#topic=3544906**)

Behavior

Or to be more specific, landing pages. Watching user metrics on your landing pages is key to understanding whether the information you're delivering matches the needs of the traffic you're receiving.

To find out what your most popular landing page is, simply click **Behavior**, then **Site Content** and then view your landing pages.

Index